Fine-Flavoured Food

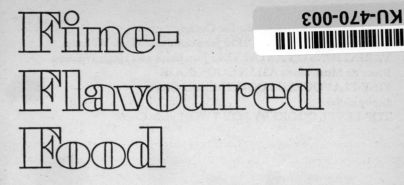

Henrietta Green has written two cookery books *Fine-Flavoured Food* and *The Marinade Cookbook*. Her cookery column 'Cooks You Can Copy' appears in *Company* magazine. She has written on food for the *Sunday Times, Financial Times, Forum* and *Taj Magazine*. A former cookery editor for *Slimmer Magazine,* she has also written on various aspects of food and cooking in *Entertaining*.

Henrietta Green

Fine-Flavoured Food

A new approach to low-fat cookery

Illustrated by Wendy Brammell

NEW ENGLISH LIBRARY/TIMES MIRROR

First published in Great Britain in 1978 by Faber & Faber Limited

Copyright © 1978 by Henrietta Green
Book design: Peter Holroyd

First NEL Paperback Edition June 1981

NEL Books are published by
New English Library Limited,
Barnard's Inn, Holborn,
London EC1N 2JR.

Typesetting by The Yale Press Limited,
London SE25.

0 450 05105 6

To my friends and family
who have eaten countless meals

Acknowledgements
I should like to thank Paula Lampard for her help in the initial preparation of this book, Andrew Hewson for his help and encouragement, Hazel Gates for typing the manuscript, Glyn Christian for advice and guidance on cheeses and whose book *Cheese and Cheesemaking* (Macdonalds Education 1977) was a fund of information; Anton Mossiman of the Dorchester Hotel and Jean Reynaud of Leith's Restaurant for contributing recipes and Elizabeth David, *Spices, Salt and Aromatics in the English Kitchen* (Penguin 1970); Peter and Joan Martin, *Japanese Cooking* (Andre Deutsch 1970); Richard Mabey, *Food for Free* (Collins 1972); Claudia Roden, *A Book of Middle Eastern Cookery* (Thomas Nelson 1968); and Jane Grigson, *Fish Cookery* (Penguin 1975), for allowing me to quote from or to refer to their respective books.

Contents

General notes

This book is based on a very simple idea—food cooked without added fat, butter, oil, cream and starch. It is a new approach to cooking and one that has long been overdue.

Attitudes to food are constantly changing and more and more people are becoming aware that our Western diet is neither particularly healthy nor well balanced. We eat too much starch, cook with too much fat and ruin the flavour of our food with heavy sauces. What is needed is a radical re-think, a change, an innovation. The answer—cooking without added fat.

There is no mystique attached to this way of cooking. It is easy and simple to follow, yet the difference in taste is remarkable. Food is lighter, cleaner and easier to digest. The full flavour of the ingredients is developed and after a while you will wonder how you could ever have cooked differently.

The difference is simply a matter of technique. Stock is used instead of oil or butter to brown or braise food, low-fat cheeses or stabilized yoghourt are added to sauces to give them a lighter, creamier taste, cultured buttermilk is whipped into soups to give them a smooth, velvety texture. Vegetables are puréed to make light, airy sauces. Meat is trimmed before cooking and no fat is added as none is necessary. Fruit is sweetened with honey or cinnamon and stewed with herbs to remove the tartness.

The recipes are not complicated to follow, but I hope you will find them delicious. Many come from abroad, France, Italy, India, China, Morocco, and I have adapted them to suit the fat-free methods. No special equipment is needed to cook them, nor should you find them any more expensive than usual.

Although it was not a prime concern, the recipes do tend to have a low-caloried content. The book, however, is not written as a book for slimmers, but rather to help and encourage you to discover a balanced yet tasty way of eating.

Introduction

Equivalent measures

Weight	Liquid
25 g = 1 oz	125 ml = $\frac{1}{4}$ pint
100 g = 4 oz	250 ml = $\frac{1}{2}$ pint
225 g = 8 oz	375 ml = $\frac{3}{4}$ pint
450 g = 1 lb	500 ml = 1 pint

Some equivalent American measures

Many of the recipes indicate quantities in teaspoons or table-spoons. English spoons vary a little in size but the approximate

American equivalents are:

1¼ US teaspoons to 1 English
1¼ US tablespoons to 1 English

The US pint is approximately five-sixths of the English pint.

Where cartons of yoghourt are indicated, these are the standard English size which contain, on average, 5 oz − that is, five-eighths of an American cup.

Although nobody seems quite clear as to when we will be going metric, to be on the safe side I have given weights and measures in both the metric and imperial systems. Actually the conversions are not strictly accurate, but for the sake of convenience I have averaged out the amounts to make the units easier to handle.

Metric recipes work on a weight unit of 25 grams which is slightly smaller than an ounce and a liquid measure of half a litre (500 ml) which is slightly less than a pint. The proportion of 25 g solid to 500 ml liquid is the same as the proportion of 1 oz to 1 pint, though the use of metric measures results in approximately a 10 per cent reduction.

One word of advice, stick to the same system throughout a recipe. Cook using either grams with litres or ounces with pints, but do not try and mix the two or change over half-way through.

The recipes will provide helpings for four to six people.

Oven temperature chart

	Gas Mark	Fahrenheit	Centigrade
Very Slow	¼	225°	110°
	½	250°	130°
Slow	1	275°	140°
	2	300°	150°
Warm	3	325°	170°
Moderate	4	350°	180°
	5	375°	190°
Fairly hot	6	400°	200°
Hot	7	425°	220°
	8	450°	230°
Very hot	9	475°	240°

Kitchen equipment

No special utensils, as such, are required for cooking in the fat-free method, as if you have a fairly well-stocked kitchen you will probably have everything that you need. However, there are certain items which make the cooking a great deal easier and these I have listed below. If you are reluctant to rush out and spend more money, do not worry, they can all be improvised from very basic equipment.

Cast-iron casserole

The one item, which I really do recommend that you buy, is a good-quality cast-iron, heavy-based enamelled casserole which can either be used on top of or in the oven. The heavy base is essential as one of the basic principles of fat-free cooking is to 'fry' or brown ingredients in stock instead of oil or butter (see page 22). Stock does not have the same ability as fat to reach a high temperature and that is why it is vital to use a good saucepan which will retain and distribute the heat evenly.

Le Creuset have an enormous range of saucepans and casseroles which are vastly superior to all other makes. They may be a little more expensive but are well worth the extra money.

Note Copper saucepans are excellent, but horribly expensive and quite a lot of trouble to keep clean. A good compromise is a copper-bottomed saucepan which has a good contact with the heat source, but is a great deal cheaper to buy.

Le Pentole

After I had finished writing *Fine-Flavoured Food* I discovered an Italian range of pans which has only just been introduced in England. The range includes various saucepans, a steamer, a bain-marie and frying pans; the pans fit on top of each other so in theory you could steam, bake and warm at the same time from one gas or electric ring.

What does make *Le Pentole* so special is that you can actually cook meat in the frying pan without adding any fat or liquid. I tested it thoroughly and believe me it is possible. The reason, according to the manufacturers, is the pan's thick base which acts as a most effective heat-conducting agent.

Made from steel, silver alloy and copper, the pans may be heavy to handle but they certainly conduct an incredible amount of heat. The base is first heated and then the meat is added; provided the base is hot enough the meat will neither stick or burn. Once it is sufficiently browned, flavourings can be added in the normal way; the pan is covered with its lid which is fitted with a vapour stop so none of the liquid can evaporate. The meat is left to cook for the appropriate time.

Before you rush out and buy *Le Pentole*, it has one disadvantage; the price. For the entire range you can expect to pay about £85.00 and for the frying/skillet pan £30.00 The Conran Shop in the Fulham Road, London is the sole stockist and I am assured that numerous sets have been sold within the first week of the range being available in this country.

Heat-diffusing mat

As it is often necessary to simmer in a small amount of liquid, a simmer-mat placed between a saucepan and the heat source will diffuse and control a low heat; and thus prevent the ingredients from burning and sticking to the bottom of the pan or drying out. Made from ridged metal, stove-enamel or asbestos, an efficient heat-diffusing mat should not cost more than around £1.50.

Meat brick

Meat or chicken cooked in a brick needs no added fat. The principle of cooking in a brick is quite straightforward. Made from an unglazed, porous clay, the brick is first soaked in water for 15 minutes before being placed in a cold oven. As the oven heats up, the warm air causes the moisture absorbed by the brick to evaporate, which in turn controls the humidity and temperature inside the brick. The meat cooks slowly and retains its juices so it will not shrink or dry out. If you want to crisp the skin, the lid of the brick can be removed a few minutes before the meat is cooked to allow the direct heat to brown it.

There are various bricks on the market, ranging from a satisfactory basic version which is sold for around £2.75 for the small size and up to £5.00 for the larger size from Habitat and most kitchenware shops, to the more ornate German version, a Romertopf, which will set you back about £6.00.

Note Meat wrapped in foil will cook without any added fat, although there will not be the same degree of temperature control and shrinkage may occur.

Fish brick

It is exactly the same as a meat brick except that it is shaped to take a whole fish. It is advisable to keep separate bricks for fish and for meat as the fish tends to flavour the clay strongly and would ruin the taste of a joint.

Note Fish wrapped in foil can be baked slowly in an oven without any added fat.

Roasting-grate

A metal roasting-grate, placed in a baking-dish, will raise and support the meat so that the fat can drain off. They are not widely available in this country (I bought mine from Richard Dare, 93 Regents Park Road, London NW1, and it cost me about £3.50) but a cake cooling rack balanced over a baking-dish will do just as well. Its only disadvantage is that you cannot angle the meat.

If you want to steam-roast the meat, fill the baking-tin with warm water, which will moisten and cook the meat as it evaporates.

Note Meat cooked on a revolving spit or suspended by meathooks from the oven shelf are similar methods.

Steamer

There are various types of steamers. The traditional Chinese steaming-baskets, made from plaited bamboo, are the most attractive and are available from Cheong Leen, 4 Tower Street, London wc2, and Wing Yip Supermarkets, 45-47 Faulkner Street, Manchester 1M1 4EE, and both shops run a mail-order service.

The most conventional metal steamers either fit on to or are lowered into a saucepan. They are made from aluminium or stainless steel and can be bought from any store or kitchenware shop and should cost between £1.00 and £2.00

Note An efficient steamer can be improvised by balancing a colander, sieve or plate over a saucepan filled with water.

Wok

Made from cast-iron or stainless steel, the wok is a Chinese frying-pan. The sides are sloped to allow the food to drain once it has been cooked. It can be bought from Chinese supermarkets or kitchenware shops.

Note A wide saucepan is an adequate substitute but the food will have to be strained and removed and kept warm separately.

Double boiler

A double saucepan is one saucepan fitted over another filled with water, so that a sauce can be stirred and cooked over a controlled heat.

Note A heatproof bowl placed in a saucepan filled with water is really all you need. Make sure that it is a tight fit otherwise you will have difficulty in gripping the bowl when beating.

Food Processors and Liquidizers

In the past few years there has been an innovation in the kitchen, a real step forward in terms of equipment – the food processor. It does everything it claims to do (it chops, shreds, minces, grates) and is especially good at puréeing. There are now several different makes on the market but the best is still the Magimix. Magimix have now introduced a cheaper version, the Robot-Chef and prices start at about £50. Less elaborate and cheaper are the various liquidizers or liquidizing attachments made by such companies as Phillips, Sunbeam, Kenwood and Moulinex. They all seem to be rather similar in quality and efficiency and will purée and liquidize satisfactorily.

At the lower end of the scale there is the hand vegetable-mouli. It comes with a choice of three blades, one for fine, one for medium and one for coarse puréeing. It works remarkably well and is a lot cheaper than an electric liquidizer.

Note Purées can also be made by pounding the ingredients through a wire or nylon sieve. This is obviously the cheapest method, but the vegetables must be well cooked otherwise they will not purée satisfactorily.

Herbs and spices and their suppliers

'She was the sweet marjoram of the salad, or, rather, the herb of grace.' (William Shakespeare, *All's Well That Ends Well.*)

We seem to have forgotten, until recently, our traditional methods of seasoning with herbs and spices. Early English cookery manuscripts are littered with recipes for meats, puddings and preserves, with cardamoms, cloves, ginger and cinnamon as essential ingredients. It was to secure a lion's share of the spice market, in order to satisfy our appetites, that the East India Trading Company was formed—the results of that venture are known only too well. Thyme, lovage, mint, rosemary and sage were also popular and gardens were full of these and many other herbs which were grown for their culinary and medicinal uses.

During the past few years there has been a revival of interest in cooking with herbs and spices; possibly as a reaction against the blandness of convenience foods or possibly as we have discovered foreign styles of cooking and rediscovered our own. The result is that most food stores now stock a wide range of the better-known herbs and spices and they are easily obtainable.

However, there are some dried herbs such as angelica, salad burnet, dill weed, juniper berries, which are often used but are quite difficult to buy. Certain health food or specialist shops may stock them, otherwise they can be obtained by mail order from Baldwins, 173 Walworth Road, London SE17. Culpepper carry most of the unusual herbs and other delicacies, like green peppercorns, green ginger in brine and a good French mustard. They have shops in London, Norwich, Cambridge, Northampton and Brighton; mail order enquiries should be addressed to Culpepper Ltd., Hadstock Road, Linton, Cambridge CB1 6NJ.

For the more exotic oriental spices, I recommend the Bombay Emporium, 70 Grafton Way, London W1, who specialize in Indian spices, and Cheong Leen, 4-10 Tower Street, London WC1, who sell everything Chinese including the famous 5-Spice Powder (a blend of star-anise, fennel seed, cinnamon, clove bud, and ginger, which is essential to Chinese cooking). Both shops deal with either personal or mail order customers.

Store your herbs and spices in airtight, clearly labelled jars and keep them within easy reach while cooking. You will find them an attractive and useful addition to your kitchen, but remember to renew them from time to time or they will have lost their flavour.

For those with the space and inclination I suggest growing a selection of your own herbs – Carter's, Sutton's and Suffolk Herbs produce a comprehensive range – or buying herb plants from a garden centre or shop and transplanting them into the garden or a window box.

Do use freshly ground black pepper as it tends to lose its pungency when stored – so it is worth while investing in a pepper-mill and grinding the pepper as you need it. Parsley should always be used fresh as a garnish. Dried parsley leaves do nothing for a dish, so either buy a small bundle from a greengrocer or a vegetable stall or try growing your own. It can be quite difficult as, according to superstition, parsley only grows in a household where the woman is master!

The measurements for herbs in the recipes are for dried herbs, so if you are using fresh, a sprig or a few leaves should be chopped finely and a slightly larger quantity used.

Sugar and sweeteners

There is a great debate taking place at the moment about the danger of using cyclamates. Whilst I admit to having no strong opinions one way or the other, I have avoided their use.

Instead, I suggest sweetening a dish with one of the following: unrefined Barbados sugar, honey, molasses, orange juice, cinnamon. Fruit stewed with certain herbs (angelica, sweet cicely or elderflower) loses its tartness, but will possibly need to be sweetened. In all the recipes the amounts used will depend on your own 'sweet tooth' and the quantities I have given are only a rough guide. If, on the other hand, you have no objection to cyclamates, by all means substitute an artificial sweetener whenever you feel like it.

Yoghourt, low-fat cheeses and cultured buttermilk

An advantage of fat-free cooking is to make creamy-textured sauces from *fromage blanc,* cottage cheese, yoghourt and buttermilk instead of using the more conventional products such as butter, milk, cream and oil which have a much higher fat and calorie content.

The fat content of a dairy product is measured as a percentage of the dry matter, not as a percentage of the whole. Strictly speaking, with the exception of the true *fromage blanc,* the rest do contain a small percentage of fat solids, but by comparison it is such a small amount that it is almost negligible.

Yoghourt

Most commercial yoghourts are made from skimmed milk and separated milk solids, with added bacteria. They have a fairly low fat content and are loosely defined as containing fat solids something less than cow's milk (3 per cent) – low-fat yoghourt has a 1 per cent fat content.

Home-made yoghourt

To make your own yoghourt, all you need is 2 teaspoons of live yoghourt to every pint of skimmed or reconstituted dried milk. Bring the milk to the boil and simmer for one minute to sterilize it. Leave it to cool until it is hand hot, so that you are able to stand your finger in it for a count of five – this takes 15 to 20 minutes. Put the live yoghourt in a bowl and slowly add the milk, beating it constantly until the two are thoroughly mixed together. Either (1) pour the contents of the bowl into a thermos flask and leave to stand for about 8 hours; or (2) cover the bowl tightly with a plastic bag and wrap in newspapers or a towel or blanket. Place it in a warm, draught-free place like an airing cupboard, on top of the hot-water tank or at the back of the Aga, and leave for 8 hours or until the yoghourt is set. If you allow the yoghourt to stand for too long it will turn sour. Keep in the fridge and use as required.

Stabilized yoghourt

Yoghourt has a tendency to curdle when boiled or baked, so it is advisable to stabilize before cooking. To save time you can stabilize a large amount and keep it in the fridge for a week or so and use when required.

500 ml (1 pint) yoghourt
1 egg white, lightly beaten
pinch of salt

Beat the yoghourt in a saucepan and stir in the egg white and salt. Gently bring to the boil, stirring constantly, with a regular action and then simmer for about 10 minutes on a very low heat (use a heat-diffusing mat if necessary) as the yoghourt must not be allowed to burn. The yoghourt will form a smooth thick paste which can then be added to meat or vegetables and reheated without any fear of curdling or separating.

Low-fat cheeses

Cottage cheese

Cottage cheese is made from skimmed milk which is set and washed to remove all traces of whey. It contains about 4 per cent or less fat solid, which compares it favourably with hard cheese. Fresh cottage cheese has a slightly gritty texture and it is advisable to pass it through a sieve before use or to give it a quick whirl in a liquidizer or food processor.

Fromage blanc

Fromage blanc is a fully skimmed-milk curd cheese which contains no fat solids. At the time of writing this book, no equivalent is manufactured in Britain, so I had to rely on imported products or make my own. Bon Blanc, Jockey and Speizequark are the best-known brands and although they are not widely distributed they are available from most specialist food shops. Check the label to make sure that you are buying the right cheese which is clearly marked at 0 per cent fat solids. All the brands also produce other curd cheeses containing 20 per cent and 40 per cent fat solids – which is about the same fat content as an ordinary hard cheese – so it can be a little confusing. If you find difficulty in buying fromage blanc you can use the following recipe to make your own quite simply, but remember that it will not be entirely fat free.

3 tablespoons cottage cheese
3 tablespoons yoghourt
dash of lemon juice (optional)

Blend the ingredients together in a liquidizer to form a smooth paste, or pass the cottage cheese through a sieve and beat in the yoghourt a little at a time until the smooth texture has been reached. A dash of lemon juice can be added to sharpen the flavour.

Fromage blanc is used instead of cream but care must be taken when adding to food to prevent it from curdling. It should not be subjected to a fierce heat and once it has been added to a sauce it is best kept warm in a double boiler.

Yoghourt cheese

This can be used in cooking instead of cottage cheese or eaten on its own mixed with freshly ground black pepper or freshly chopped herbs.

500 ml (1 pint) yoghourt
1 teaspoon salt

Stir the salt into the yoghourt and mix together. Pour the yoghourt into a colander lined with a piece of damp muslin or cheesecloth and leave to drain overnight. The whey will separate leaving a soft creamy cheese.

Other low-fat cheeses

Ricotta, an Italian curd cheese, Mizerette, the Greek version, and ordinary low-fat curd cheese all contain a higher proportion of fat—up to 10 per cent. They are still preferable to cream or butter, but should be avoided unless absolutely necessary.

Cultured buttermilk

Cultured buttermilk is the by-product of churning cream to make butter; it has been cultured to replace some of the bacteria lost during pasteurization. It has a low-fat content, between 1·1 per cent to 1·2 per cent fat solid, and a smooth velvety texture which makes it ideal for adding to soups and sauces. Raine's are the main distributors and should you have any difficulty in obtaining their product, write to Raine's Dairy Foods, 15-21 Northwold Road, London N16, for a list of suppliers. Failing that, use yoghourt instead, it has a sharper flavour, but is the only low-fat substitute.

Stocks

A good stock is particularly important to the fat-free way of cooking, so I have given it a special section to itself. It is used instead of butter and oil to seal meat, to braise vegetables and as the base of many soups and sauces. Once you start cooking the fat-free way, you will realize that you do not need any additional fats and, moreover, you will notice a difference in the food: it is lighter, easier to digest and has a cleaner and more definite flavour.

Obviously it matters what ingredients you use for any recipe, but it is even more important in this method of cooking. The better the raw products, the better the end result. That is why I advise you to make your own stock. I have nothing against stock cubes; they are convenient, easy to use and to prepare and ideal in emergencies, but if it is flavour you are after, nothing beats good, home-made stock. One of the good things about making your own stock is that you can use up all your left-overs and trimmings. I use whatever happens to be around in the kitchen: vegetable parings, leek tops, giblets, bacon rind, meat, bones and even fruit peel. If you do include any root vegetables (parsnips, swedes and turnips) you must boil up the stock every day otherwise they will turn it sour, so it is perhaps easier to leave them out altogether. I have selected three basic recipes for stock: meat, chicken and fish. What you choose to add to them will depend on what is currently in season and what you have to use up in your kitchen.

If you make a lot of stock, it is worth your while investing in a proper stockpot, a heavy enamelled iron or steel pan with straight sides and a tight-fitting lid is most suitable. If the stockpot is too shallow, the liquid will evaporate while cooking – that is why I prefer the heavy-based, tall pots, as they also retain the heat most efficiently. The stock must be well and truly skimmed, leaving as little fat as possible. This is done by bringing all the ingredients to the boil and removing the scum that has risen to the surface. The heat is then turned down and the stock left to simmer. If it is boiled too fiercely, not only will too much liquid evaporate, but also the scum will dissolve as it rises to the surface and make the stock cloudy. The stock should be skimmed throughout the cooking, but always remember to replace the stockpot lid. Once the stock is cooked, it is passed through a sieve and the ingredients should be pressed with a wooden spoon or press to make sure that all their goodness is extracted. The strained stock is cooled before use, allowing the remaining fat to collect at the surface. This layer can be scooped off or, if it is broken up and difficult to handle, try soaking it up with an absorbent paper like ordinary kitchen roll or a brown paper bag.

To store the stock, either keep it in a jug in the fridge and use it as required, or reduce it by boiling it vigorously in an uncovered saucepan after it has been strained, and then freeze it in individual ice-cube trays. These cubes are easy to handle and the concentrated stock will melt if you simply heat it up in a saucepan or pour hot water over it.

Stock should be seasoned after it is made. As it is used for such a variety of purposes, it makes sense to adjust the seasoning according to the purpose for which it is required. Also, regardless of whatever saucepan you use, some evaporation is bound to take place and the flavour might end up far too concentrated. The simplest way of avoiding this danger is to add the salt at a later stage.

One last word. By adding a few vegetables and heating them in the stock you have a nourishing dish – a good stock is a soup in itself.

Browning food in stock

I cannot stress too much the importance of stock to the fat-free way of cooking. One of the basic principles is to braise or brown ingredients in stock instead of oil or butter. The stock must be heated until bubbling so that its effect is similar to that of hot fat. Only a small amount of stock should be used initially; once the ingredients are added, they must be stirred constantly so that they do not stick to the bottom of the pan.

Onions, garlic and spices should be cooked until soft to release their flavour, and then the remaining ingredients can be added according to the recipe. Meat can be browned in a small amount of stock, but care must be taken to turn it frequently so that it does not burn.

Basic meat stock

As in all the recipes for stock, I use a bouquet garni for flavouring. Opinions seem to vary as to exactly what herbs should be included in a bouquet garni, but I make mine from fresh or dried marjoram, thyme, parsley and a bay leaf, tied together in a small square of muslin. The advantage is that it is discarded after cooking and so no little bits of herbs are floating in the stock. Prepared bouquets garni can be bought in packets from most supermarkets and good grocery stores, but I think they are exorbitantly priced.

1 kg (2 lb) meat bones (see note below)	2 large onions
	bacon rind
2 large carrots	6 peppercorns
1 bouquet garni	water to cover

To make a brown stock, the bones should first be browned in the pan with a little water. Then add the other ingredients and any other trimmings which may come to hand. Bring to the boil, skim and leave to simmer for 1½-2 hours.

Note Beef bones make a stronger and less greasy stock than lamb bones. Veal knuckles boiled with carrots and a glass of white wine give a particularly delicate flavour.

Basic chicken stock

It seems rather extravagant to use a raw chicken carcass to make a stock – unless of course you happen to be boning a chicken – but if you simmer raw giblets with a cooked carcass you will get a real chicken-flavoured stock.

chicken carcass and giblets	1 bouquet garni (see note overleaf)
1 large onion, roughly chopped	6 peppercorns
2 carrots, scraped and chopped	1-2 litres (2-4 pints) water, to
1 stick of celery and celery tops	cover
handful of parsley stalks	

Pick the carcass clean, removing all skin as it makes the stock rather fatty. Put all the ingredients in a stockpot, cover with water, and bring to the boil. Remove the scum, cover and simmer for a further 1–2 hours, skimming constantly. Strain through a sieve and set aside to cool. Remove fat and store as suggested on page 23.

Note The zest of a lemon can be added while cooking – it gives the stock a slightly tangy flavour and I also find it makes a pleasant change to use lemon thyme or lemon balm instead of a bouquet garni.

Fish stock

Ask your fishmonger for any trimmings, bones, skin and heads. Most shops are kind enough to give them away free, but even if you do have to pay, it is still worth it. Unfortunately, fish stock does not keep for more than two days unless frozen, but it is quick and easy to make.

½-1 kg (1-2 lb) fish trimmings
1 large onion, sliced
3 or 4 parsley stalks
1 carrot, sliced
bay leaf

blade of mace
zest of lemon peel
6 peppercorns
1 glass dry white wine
water

The danger of making a fish stock is to cook it for too long, thus making it resemble an unpleasant pot of glue! Should you want to reduce the stock, strain it and remove the fish trimmings first. Put all the ingredients in a pan, pour in enough water to cover and slowly bring to the boil. Remove the scum and leave to simmer for about half an hour. Strain through a fine sieve which can, if necessary, be lined with muslin, to catch the small bones.

The first course

The serving of the first course is left over from the days when meals were far more elaborate than they are now. It was not until the nineteenth century that the order of courses was formalized. Up until then, meals had tended to be rather higgledy-piggledy affairs bearing little resemblance to the order of courses we know of today. Dishes were brought to the table as and when they were ready and there seemed to be no progression of tastes.

Mrs Beeton, however, in the *Book of Household Management*, had very definite ideas about how a dinner should be served. Soup was usually the first course although 'Now [it] is very often preceded by such little dishes as caviare, croutons, oysters and other little appetisans.' It was followed by a fish, but great care must be taken as 'you do not want your fish ready before the soup, causing the former to look flabby and most likely to break and lose their trim appearance.' Then came the entrée or made dishes, followed by joints and poultry, etc., then sweets, cheese, cooked and uncooked, or such small savouries. Times and budgets have obviously changed since guests sat down to that kind of meal, and meals and dinner parties are no longer the rigid occasions they were, when families and guests had to assemble before being ushered into the sanctity of the dining-room.

None the less, I think that if you can find the time, it is well worth making a first course. Somehow it does get the meal off to a good start and make it more of an occasion. Soups, vegetables, pâtés, mousses and egg dishes all make good starters, and in most cases can be prepared in advance.

Soups

'Soup of the evening, O beautiful soup', wrote Lewis Caroll in *Alice in Wonderland,* and how right he was. Thick or thin, hot or cold, a good soup will satisfy the most demanding of appetites.

My enthusiasm for soup-making grew with my collection of Victorian soup plates – the old-fashioned, full-rimmed and delicately decorated china kind – which laid out on a table, filled to the brim with steaming soup, are a joy and inspiration to any 'soupier'. Believe it or not, I can still pick them up at junk shops or jumble sales for under 50p.

Like my many-patterned plates there are many different soups, in fact most countries boast a national soup. Russia has its Bortsch, Italy the Minestrone, China has a choice of Shark's Fin Soup and Bird's Nest Soup. In Wales it is Leek Soup, and in Scotland the Scotch Broth – a thick nourishing soup heavily laced with mutton. Each soup reflects the tastes, produce and cooking methods of its country of origin and, like our own Brown Windsor, has become a national symbol.

Soups have been made for centuries and are one of the earliest known methods of cooking. As food and its preparation became more sophisticated, the soup was frowned on and thought to be no more than 'peasants' gruel'; it was not until the nineteenth century, that it was considered fit to be served in polite society and once more included in the menu.

Nowadays many a household serves a soup with salad as a complete meal. A soup is a wholesome cheap way of feeding the family, it can make a nourishing meal or an appetizing starter and is an economical way of using up left-overs – meat, fish or vegetables. Even their cooking water can be absorbed into a warm and welcome stockpot soup.

There is no mystique about making a good soup – it is as good as your ingredients. Mrs Beeton sets out 'certain facts which a good soup maker must act on'. They are helpful hints and so I have listed them as follows: (1) Slow cooking is essential for most soups. (I often put a soup on the bottom shelf of the oven if I happen to be roasting or baking at the same time – it saves a great deal of fuel and then I leave it to cook as the oven cools down.) (2) Soup can be made from anything – fish, flesh or fruit. (Mrs Beeton mentions flour, but I have discounted it for the purposes of this book.) (3) A combination of things generally produces a better result than the use of one or two materials only—a valuable point to remember when using up left-over scraps for the household soup.

I have included recipes for different types of soup, thin and thick or purée. Thin soup is rather like a consommé; use a well-flavoured stock and serve with shredded vegetables or meat. Thick soup relies on a thickening agent to give it body and texture. The vegetables can be reduced to a pulp – puréed – and returned to the soup, or various liaisons can be beaten into the pan. In the case of puréeing the ingredients, I find that the amazing French machine the Magimix really does work wonders. It reduces the contents to a pulp in seconds. However, it is expensive to buy and a vegetable mouli, wire sieve or small liquidizer will perform the same job adequately. For a liaison I suggest egg yolks, buttermilk or stabilized yoghourt; but great care must be taken to remove the soup from direct heat and to cool slightly before beating them in. Also the soup can be re-heated but on no account should it be left to boil as it will curdle and separate.

Soups can be frozen and do freeze very well. It is advisable, however, to leave out the eggs or dairy products – these can be added when the soup is ready to be served. Soup looks very attractive garnished with freshly chopped herbs or a dusting of black pepper, which provide a good colour contrast. In the words of an eminent Victorian dietician who urged us to enjoy and savour our soup, I can strongly recommend it as 'the proper stimulant with which to start a meal'.

Tomato soup

A traditional method of making tomato soup, I have tried this recipe several times and I can heartily recommend it. If you prefer, substitute chicken for the ham, in which case add a little extra salt. 'Slice two large onions into a saucepan, with two turnips, two carrots and five or six outer sticks of celery. Put with these 4 oz [100 g] lean ham, cut into dice, and a small amount of water and steam them over a gentle fire for half an hour. Pour over them 2 quarts [2 litres] of stock in which meat has been boiled, and add six or eight ripe tomatoes. Let all simmer gently together for a couple of hours. Rub the vegetables through a sieve and boil them again with the liquor for a few minutes, add pepper and salt to taste, and serve very hot.' (Cassell's *Dictionary of Cookery*, 1893.)

Note For an even richer flavour, use less stock; about 1½ litres (3 pints) is more than adequate for six people.

Tomato and pepper soup

I find that unless I can buy really sweet full-flavoured tomatoes, preferably the fat Moroccan ones, it is better to use tinned tomatoes in soup. It is also a lot cheaper!

1 large tin, 396 g (14 oz) tomatoes	pinch of chilli powder
2 medium green peppers	1 teaspoon molasses
1 clove garlic, crushed with salt	water
1 tablespoon tomato purée	salt and pepper

Prepare the peppers by scooping out the insides, discarding the seeds and cutting into fine strips. Mix the tomato purée with a little water and heat in a saucepan. Add the garlic, chopped peppers and chilli powder and cook gently for a few minutes. Pass the contents of the tin of tomatoes through a sieve, pressing the tomatoes hard so as to remove any lumps, and stir into the saucepan. Add the molasses, cover and simmer for about 15 minutes. Adjust the seasoning and serve with freshly ground black pepper.

Gazpacho

Gazpacho is an ideal cold summer soup. It should be prepared well in advance and then chilled in the fridge. Just before serving, float a few ice cubes in the bowl, they will keep the soup really cool and help to thin it down.

450 g (1 lb) tomatoes	pinch of cayenne pepper
½ cucumber	1 tablespoon wine vinegar
1 green pepper	2 tins, 540 g (19 fl oz) each, tomato
1 small onion	juice
2 cloves garlic	salt and pepper

To peel the tomatoes plunge them in boiling water for one minute and then briefly refresh them with cold water. The skins will then be loosened. In a large bowl peel and chop the tomatoes until they are like a rough purée. Peel and dice the cucumber, onion and pepper and stir in with the tomatoes. Pound the garlic with a pinch of salt and mix in with the diced vegetables. Pour in the tomato juice, vinegar, and spinkle with cayenne pepper and freshly ground black pepper. Stir all the ingredients together and chill for at least three hours before eating.

Note If you have an opened bottle of wine handy, substitute half a glass for the vinegar.

Watercress and tomato soup

1 large bunch watercress	½ teaspoon winter savory
225 g (8 oz) tomatoes, peeled and roughly chopped	1 litre (2 pints) tomato juice
225 g (8 oz) leeks, sliced	salt and pepper

Wash the watercress and pick off the leaves and stems. Set aside a few leaves for garnish. Heat a small amount of the tomato juice in a heavy-based enamelled pan until amost boiling and cook the leeks, stirring continuously so that they do not stick to the pan. When soft add the watercress, winter savory and the fresh tomatoes. Simmer for a few minutes and then pour in the remainder of the tomato juice. Cook on a low heat until all the vegetables are quite tender. Purée the soup through a sieve or in a liquidizer and return to the saucepan. Adjust the seasoning. For the garnish, blanch the watercress leaves which you have set aside in boiling water for half a minute, drain and refresh in cold water. Serve the soup decorated with the leaves floating on the top.

Onion soup

Bowls of onion soup were always served throughout the night at Les Halles, the one-time bustling vegetable market of Paris. Most porters carried a hip-flask of cognac to keep them going during their hard shift, so the most natural thing was to add a nip to the warming soup.

450 g (1 lb) onions	1 teaspoon chopped parsley
2–3 cloves garlic, peeled and coarsely chopped	2 tablespoons brandy
grated rind and juice of 1 orange	1¼ litres (2½ pints) well-flavoured beef stock
100 g (4 oz) carton cottage cheese	salt and pepper
1 bay leaf	

Peel and slice the onions into rings. Heat a small amount of stock until boiling and cook the onion, garlic and bay leaf until soft. Stir in the grated orange rind and about two-thirds of the orange juice, and simmer for 5 minutes. Add the remainder of the stock, bring the soup to the boil, cover and simmer for a further 30-45 minutes. Remove the bay leaf and add the brandy and adjust the seasoning. Meanwhile, to prepare the topping, pound the cottage cheese with the parsley, salt and pepper and the remainder of the orange juice. Float the mixture on top of the soup and heat under a hot grill until it starts to brown. Serve immediately.

Spinach soup

Spinach, unless you use young and fresh leaves, can sometimes taste a little bitter. If this is the case, add half a peeled pear when liquidizing the spinach—it will make all the difference.

1 kg (2 lb) spinach, *or* large packet frozen spinach
1 tablespoon dill
2 hard-boiled eggs, chopped
juice of half a lemon

1 carton cultured buttermilk
1¼ litres (2½ pints) stock (chicken or light meat)
salt and pepper

Wash the spinach thoroughly, any trace of grit is guaranteed to spoil the soup, and discard the badly bruised leaves. Tear the leaves into small pieces and put into a pan. Sprinkle with salt and cook without any extra water for about 7-10 minutes. When cooked, drain the spinach and purée in a liquidizer or a vegetable mouli. Return to the pan, add the dill and stock and simmer gently for about 15 minutes. Remove from the heat and carefully beat in the buttermilk and adjust the seasoning. Serve each portion garnished with the chopped egg mixed with an extra pinch of dill.

Sorrel, lettuce and chervil soup

Mrs Beeton is rather scathing about sorrel. She found the acid very 'prononcé' and wrote: 'At the present day, English cooking is not much indebted to this plant, although the French make use of it to a considerable extent.' She was often rather suspicious of foreign foods.

100 g (4 oz) sorrel
½ small lettuce (use only inner leaves)
1 heaped teaspoon chervil
2 egg yolks

1¼ litres (2½ pints) good stock
salt and pepper
water

Wash the sorrel and lettuce discarding any bruised leaves. In a heavy pan sweat the sorrel, lettuce and chervil in a little stock until tender. Like spinach they give off plenty of water as they cook so only a small amount of stock is needed initially. Add the rest of the stock and simmer covered for a further half hour. When cooked remove the pan from the heat and allow the soup to cool. Beat the egg yolks with a tablespoon of water and then add a few spoonfuls of soup to the eggs. Then slowly pour the mixture into the soup beating continuously. The soup must not be too hot or it will curdle. Heat the soup gently, stirring continuously but do not allow to boil. Serve immediately.

Cream of cauliflower soup

This is a particularly creamy soup adapted from a French recipe. Originally it was thickened by beating in egg yolks, but I have found that the buttermilk gives it a lighter touch. Do make sure that you use a firm, fresh cauliflower, as once they go soft, cauliflowers tend to turn slightly bitter and so ruin the flavour of the soup.

1 large firm cauliflower	750 ml (1½ pints) stock (chicken or
pinch of nutmeg	vegetable)
1 carton cultured buttermilk	salt to taste
water	

Clean the cauliflower, remove the outer leaves and break up into small pieces or florets. Cook these in slightly salted boiling water until soft. Drain and add the cooking water to the rest of the stock. Pound the cauliflower to a purée and return it to the saucepan. Pour in the stock, add a pinch of nutmeg, and extra salt if necessary. Simmer for about 15 minutes and then remove from the heat. Allow it to cool and then pour in the buttermilk, beating vigorously with a balloon whisk. Gently re-heat taking great care that the soup does not boil and so curdle the buttermilk.

Avgolemono

A Greek soup which means egg and lemon. Avgolemono is usually made with chicken stock, but Jane Grigson recommends in *Fish Cookery* that you use a good fish stock or fumet. Either way it makes a most refreshing soup.

juice and grated rind of 1 lemon
2 eggs
1 litre (2 pints) chicken or fish stock

Heat the stock until almost boiling. Beat the eggs in a bowl together with the lemon juice and grated rind. Add about 2 tablespoons of stock to the eggs, beating constantly. Pour this mixture into the saucepan with the stock and continue beating. Cook over a very low flame, stirring continuously until the soup thickens; serve immediately.

Note If you have trouble controlling the flame, use an asbestos or metal heat-diffusing mat under the saucepan. On no account must the soup boil as the eggs will curdle.

Carrot and cardamom soup

This combination of flavours was inspired by a sticky, brightly coloured Indian sweet, on sale at the bazaars in North India, carrot halva. The cardamoms were used to counteract the heaviness of the ghee (clarified butter) but I liked the blend of flavours so much that I decided to adapt them to a soup.

450 g (1 lb) carrots, peeled
  and chopped
1 medium onion, finely chopped
6 cardamom pods
1 bay leaf

1 litre (2 pints) chicken stock
salt and pepper to taste
juice and grated rind of 2
  oranges
1 orange, peeled and sliced

Crush the cardamom pods with a pestle so that the little black seeds are released. Sweat the pods and seeds with the onion and grated orange rind in a little stock until the onions are almost transparent. Add the carrots, bay leaf and the rest of the chicken stock and cook for 30 minutes or until the carrots are soft. Remove the cardamom pods and the bay leaf and pass the soup through a sieve or purée in a liquidizer. Return to the pan. Adjust the seasoning and gently reheat the soup, adding the orange juice. Serve garnished with slices of fresh orange.

Beetroot and fennel soup

This soup is an adaptation of the Russian Bortsch, a richly purple beetroot soup with a sour, sharp flavour, a distinctive taste much favoured by the Slavs.

3 large uncooked beetroot
1 large fennel bulb
grated rind of 1 lemon
squeeze of lemon juice

1 carton low-fat yoghourt
1 litre (2 pints) stock
salt and pepper to taste

This soup depends on using a really rich stock. I have cooked it with both a beef and a chicken stock and a Russian cook even suggested making it with fish stock.

Wash and clean the beetroot and fennel and grate finely. Heat the stock and pour a small amount into a saucepan. Add the fennel and beetroot and cook over a low heat until all the stock has been absorbed. Stir in more stock and repeat the process at least three times until the beetroot is tender. Pour in the remainder of the stock, cover and simmer for about 20 minutes. Just before it is cooked, adjust the seasoning and add the grated lemon rind and a squeeze of lemon juice. Serve either hot or cold with a tablespoon of yoghourt floating on the surface of each bowl.

Chrysanthemum soup

The English used to flavour and decorate their food with flowers; rose petals, nasturtiums, marigolds and violets were commonly used. Sadly, this custom seems to have been long forgotten and it is left to the Chinese, who still retain the art, to make chrysanthemum soup. Rather than go to the trouble of making and clarifying a consommé, I would suggest that you use a good tinned variety for this recipe.

2 slices ham, finely sliced
2 spring onions, finely chopped
small tin, 269 g (9½ oz), water
  chestnuts, drained and chopped
1 large chrysanthemum flower

2 tins, 425 g (15 oz) each,
  consommé
1 tablespoon dry sherry
1 teaspoon soya sauce
salt and pepper to taste

Heat the consommé until almost boiling. Stir in the sherry and soya sauce. Add the ham, water chestnuts and spring onions, taking care to separate all the ingredients out. Remove the petals carefully from a chrysanthemum flower and float on top of the soup. Simmer for a further minute and serve immediately.

Jerusalem artichoke soup

The Jerusalem artichoke did not originate from the Holy City, nor has it ever grown there. The name is a corruption of the Italian *girasole articiocco*—the sunflower artichoke—which translated literally means artichoke turning to the sun.

450 g (1 lb) Jerusalem artichokes
2 medium onions, finely chopped
1 teaspoon chervil
juice of half a lemon

750 ml (1½ pints) chicken stock or
  water
salt and pepper to taste
1 teaspoon parsley

Peel and slice the artichokes and soak them in lemon juice, diluted with a tablespoon of water, to prevent them from discolouring and going brown before cooking. When ready, drain and place in a saucepan with the onions, stock, chervil and salt and pepper. Bring to the boil and simmer gently for about 20 minutes or until the artichokes are soft. Reduce the ingredients to a pulp by pressing through a fine sieve or purée in a liquidizer. Add a squeeze of lemon juice and adjust the seasoning. The soup has a soft velvety consistency and looks particularly appetizing garnished with freshly chopped parsley.

Eliza Acton's apple soup

Miss Acton's delicious spiced apple soup is best made with cooking applies if you like a slightly tart flavour.

325 g (12 oz) cooking apples   1 litre (2 pints) strong beef stock
½ teaspoon ground ginger   salt and pepper to taste

Wash and chop the apples without removing the peel or core.
Heat the stock and add the apples to the pan. Cover and simmer
the soup until the apples are tender. Pass the soup through a
sieve, pressing the apples hard so that they are reduced to a fine
pulp – I find that a wooden fruit press is ideal for this. Discard the
cores and pips. Mix the ground ginger with the soup and give it a
vigorous stir so that all the ingredients combine. Adjust the
seasoning and reheat the soup. A variation is to substitute a
heaped teaspoon of freshly chopped mint for the ground ginger.

Celery and almond soup

1 head of celery   ½ teaspoon turmeric
1 leek   1 litre (2 pints) chicken stock
1 medium onion   salt and pepper to taste
25 g (1 oz) ground almonds   1 teaspoon flaked almonds

Wash the vegetables and chop roughly, discarding the green leek
tops and the celery leaves. Heat a small amount of the stock with
the turmeric and cook the vegetables, stirring continuously until
soft. Pour in the remainder of the stock, cover and simmer for
about 20 minutes until the vegetables are thoroughly cooked.
Purée the soup in a liquidizer or vegetable mouli, then pass
through a sieve making sure that you remove all the strings from
the celery. Return to the saucepan and stir in the ground
almonds. Gently heat the soup – the longer it is left to cook, the
stronger the taste of the almonds; and serve garnished with
toasted flaked almonds.

Iced pickled cucumber soup

This soup makes a pleasant change from the better-known
Tzatziki, the Greek soup made from fresh cucumbers, garlic, dill
and yoghourt. For the pickled version, I prefer the Polish dill
cucumbers which are bottled by Krakus, although I have made
the soup with my own home-made variety (see page 139) or with

the New Green cucumbers available from most Jewish delicatessen. Each version has a different flavour so I can only suggest that you experiment for yourself.

225 g (8 oz) pickled cucumber
  (Krakus Polish)
pinch of mace
pinch of ginger
pinch of allspice
1 tablespoon fresh dill or fennel

1 teaspoon honey
1 carton low-fat yoghourt
1 litre (2 pints) good stock, chicken
  or light meat
salt and pepper to taste

Roughly chop the pickled cucumbers and simmer covered in the stock for about half an hour. Pass through a sieve or purée them and return to the pan with the stock. Stir in the spices, the honey and plenty of freshly ground pepper. Simmer for a further 10 minutes and then remove from the heat. Chill in the fridge for a minimum of 3 hours. Just before serving, stir in the carton of yoghourt and sprinkle with the fresh chopped dill or fennel.

Curry soup

Really more a meal than a starter, curry soup is my 'using up cooked left-overs broth'. Each year I make it with the scraps from the Christmas turkey; but chicken, pork, beef, or any vegetables will do just as well.

225 g (8 oz) chopped meat
1 medium onion, finely chopped
1 clove garlic, chopped
1 teaspoon tomato purée
pinch of garam masala

pinch of turmeric
pinch of ground cinnamon
1 bay leaf
1 litre (2 pints) good stock
salt and pepper

Mix the tomato purée and the cinnamon with a tablespoon of water and heat until bubbling in a heavy-based enamelled saucepan. Stir in the garam masala and turmeric and cook for a few minutes, stirring continuously so that the spices do not burn or stick to the bottom of the pan. The spices must be fiercely cooked to remove their raw taste. Add the onion, garlic, bay leaf and more stock as required and cook until tender. Stir in the meat and whatever left-overs you may want to use and pour in the rest of the stock. Adjust the seasoning, cover and simmer for about 15 minutes.

Note A few tomatoes dropped in whole and simmered for about 10 minutes give the soup a dash of colour.

Mussel soup

The rich man who called a mussel, 'the poor man's oyster' did not know what he was missing. They are simply delicious, succulent and juicy, their bright orange beads of flesh just waiting to be swallowed. Do be careful to discard any dead or open specimens and to clean them thoroughly according to the instructions on page 53.

2 litres (4 pints) mussels
100 g (4 oz) mushrooms, finely chopped
1 onion, finely sliced
2 leeks, finely sliced
large pinch of oregano

1 bay leaf
1 carton stabilized yoghourt (p.19)
2 glasses dry white wine
water
salt and pepper

Scrub the mussels and remove their barnacles and beards with a sharp knife. Discard open ones. In a large saucepan, heat 125 ml (¼ pint) of water with one glass of dry white wine; put in the mussels, cover and simmer for 5–7 minutes until they are all open. Discard closed ones. Strain the mussels, keeping the liquid, and when cool enough to handle, separate the mussels from their shells and roughly chop. Line a sieve with a piece of muslin or kitchen paper and pour the cooking-liquor through, so that the grit is thoroughly strained. Add the second glass of wine and enough water to make it up to 1 litre (2 pints). Heat a small amount of the liquid and cook the leeks and onions with the oregano and bay leaf until soft. Purée the vegetables and return to the pan. Pour the remainder of the stock into the pan with the mussels and mushrooms and simmer for 5–10 minutes. Adjust the seasoning and just before serving stir in the yoghourt.

Fish soup

Fish soup is a firm favourite. Most fish, either fresh- or sea-water can be used. In fact, the wider the variety, the tastier the soup. A touch of saffron makes all the difference – ground Spanish, which is much cheaper, will suffice for this recipe.

1¼-2 kg (3-4 lb) lean fish (cod, haddock, hake, squid, whiting, shellfish, rock salmon, etc.)
2 leeks, chopped
2 cloves garlic, crushed with salt
1 small tin, 226 g (8 oz) tomatoes
1 teaspoon summer savory
salt and pepper to taste
1 teaspoon thyme
pinch of saffron
1 bay leaf
1 small piece orange peel
1½ litres (3 pints) water
freshly chopped parsley

To prepare the fish, wash, clean and scale and cut into rough slices. The heads and trimmings can either be added to the soup or saved for a fish stock. In a tablespoon of the tomato juice drained from the tin, sweat the leeks and garlic until almost transparent. Pour in the remainder of the tomatoes and the juice and add the orange peel and herbs. Cook for a few minutes and stir in the fish. Cover and simmer for 5 minutes and then pour in the water. Boil uncovered for about 30 to 40 minutes. About 10 minutes before it is ready add the saffron as it should never be over-cooked. Adjust the seasoning and serve immediately garnished with the freshly chopped parsley.

Other first course dishes

As a general rule I try not to serve two fish or meat courses, but it does not really matter provided there is a variety of flavours and the dishes complement each other.

Vegetables make a light and tasty appetizer, as do egg dishes. Pâtés and mousses are firm favourites and can usually be prepared in advance.

Most of these recipes also make good lunch dishes and are ideal to take on a picnic on a warm summer's day.

Stuffed artichokes

The globe artichoke is one of the world's oldest cultivated vegetables. Theophrastus wrote in the fourth century BC, 'the head of Scolymusis [artichoke] most pleasant, being boyled or eaten raw, but chiefly when it is in flower, as also the inner substance of the heads is eaten.'

4 globe artichokes
half a lemon
water
salt to taste

Stuffing:
50 g (2 oz) cooked tongue, finely diced

2 tomatoes, peeled and chopped
1 small onion, finely chopped
1 teaspoon capers
1 teaspoon mixed herbs
1 carton *fromage blanc* (p.20)
juice of half a lemon
salt and pepper to taste

To prepare the artichokes, wash in salted water. Trim the leaves with a pair of scissors and cut off the stalks level with the base so that they can stand upright. Rub the leaves with a piece of lemon to prevent discolouring and plunge the artichokes into boiling salted water. Cook for about 45 minutes or until the leaves can be easily pulled away and the flesh is quite soft. Drain and leave to cool.

Mix all the ingredients for the stuffing together and set half the quantity aside. To stuff the artichokes pull out the centre leaves and scoop out the thistle-like choke. Spoon the stuffing into the centre and replace the leaves. Pour the remaining half of the stuffing over the artichokes and serve.

Courgettes with pine kernels

Pine nuts or kernels are quite delicious. They come from the *Pinus pinea* which grows in the Mediterranean countries and although now imported into this country, the nuts or *pinoli* can still be quite hard to track down. Most health food shops or continental delicatessen are starting to stock them, but I warn you that they are rather expensive. If you cannot find them or are reluctant to pay the price, use unsalted flaked almonds or chopped hazelnuts instead.

450g (1 lb) courgettes
50 g (2 oz) pine kernels
1 teaspoon Moutarde de Meaux
  (or any herbal mustard)

juice of half a lemon
1 carton cultured buttermilk
salt and pepper to taste

Wash and dry the courgettes and cut into 1-inch thick slices. Heat enough water to cover the bottom of the saucepan and put in the courgettes. Cover and simmer gently for a few minutes until they are cooked but still quite crisp. Meanwhile roast the pine kernels in a warm oven, Gas Mark 3, 325° F or 170° C, for about 15–20 minutes, shaking them occasionally in the dish so that they brown on all sides. Drain the courgettes and arrange in a flat dish. Mix the buttermilk with the lemon juice, mustard, salt and pepper to taste. Add the pine kernels to the courgettes and pour over the seasoned buttermilk. Leave to marinade in a cool place for about 2 to 3 hours before serving.

Tomato tarts

English tomatoes, unless they are home-grown, are rarely sweet enough to make a rich filling. So, by way of compensation, I add either a teaspoon of tomato purée or a teaspoon of molasses.

675 g (1½ lb) tomatoes
8–10 large cabbage leaves
1 onion, finely chopped
1 clove garlic, crushed
1 bay leaf
1 teaspoon basil

pinch of nutmeg
1 teaspoon molasses, *or* 1 teaspoon
  tomato purée (optional)
1 teaspoon tomato juice
salt and pepper to taste

Roughly chop the tomatoes and put them in a heavy-based enamelled pan with the onion, garlic, bay leaf, basil and tomato juice and molasses or tomato purée if required. Simmer over a gentle heat, stirring occasionally until they have reduced to a thick pulp and all the excess liquid has evaporated. Remove the bay leaf and press the pulp through a sieve. Adjust the seasoning. Lightly oil a quiche dish or cake tin and line with the cabbage leaves, making sure they overlap and that they are long enough to fold over the filling. Spoon the mixture into the centre and spread it over the base of the dish. Tuck the cabbage leaves over the top and sprinkle with a little pepper and a pinch of nutmeg. Bake in a moderate oven, Gas Mark 5, 375° F, 190° C, for about 25 minutes until the cabbage is crisp but not dry.

Baked mushrooms

I have never had any luck in gathering wild mushrooms. I did once find a field carpeted with them, only to discover after a stint of back-breaking picking that they were crawling with maggots.

However, all mushrooms, cultivated or wild – with the exception of morels – should be exposed to as little water as possible and should never be peeled. All they need is a quick rub with a damp cloth and any blemishes can be cut off with a sharp knife.

225 g (8 oz) medium-sized mushrooms	½ teaspoon thyme
	juice of half a lemon
½ teaspoon basil	salt and cayenne pepper to taste
½ teaspoon marjoram	1 carton stabilized yoghourt (p.19)

Wipe the mushrooms with a damp cloth and discard the base of the stalks. Cut the mushrooms into quarters and put them in a shallow baking dish. Mix the yoghourt with the herbs and lemon juice and pour it over the mushrooms. Bake in a warm oven, Gas Mark 3, 325°F, 170°C, for about 15 minutes or until the mushrooms are cooked but still quite firm. Serve hot or cold, dusted with a coating of cayenne pepper.

Crudité

A dish piled high with crisp raw vegetables surrounding a dip –
what better way to start a meal. The idea is to cut up a colourful
array–carrots, fennel, florets of cauliflower, cucumber or whatever you prefer – and arrange them on a large plate, around a dip.
Take a vegetable and plunge it into a dip. The dips are simple to
make and I have included a few variations.

Curried cheese

100 g (4 oz) cottage cheese
2 teaspoons egg sauce (p.133)

1 teaspoon curry powder
salt to taste

Pass the cottage cheese through a sieve into a bowl. Stir in the egg
sauce and curry powder. Add salt to taste.

Egg mix

3 eggs
¼ cucumber
½ teaspoon dill

½ carton cultured buttermilk
salt and pepper to taste

Hard-boil the eggs and plunge immediately into cold water to prevent the yolks discolouring. Peel and halve the eggs and remove
the yolks. Chop the whites and pass the yolks through a sieve. Peel
and dice the cucumber and mix all the ingredients together in a
bowl. Add salt and pepper to taste.

Aubergine mix

1 large aubergine
1 clove garlic, finely crushed
1 teaspoon mint

1 carton low-fat yoghourt
salt and pepper to taste

Wash and dry the aubergine. Either roast it whole in a fairly hot
oven, Gas Mark 5, 375°F, 190°C, for about 20-30 minutes or cook
it over an open gas flame, turning it constantly so that the skin
chars but does not burn. Peel and mash, discarding the stalk and

core, and mix the garlic, chopped mint and yoghourt, with the aubergine. Adjust the seasoning and chill before serving.

Raita

½ cucumber	1 carton low-fat yoghourt
1 teaspoon mint	salt to taste
pinch paprika	

Peel and coarsely grate the cucumber. Mix together with the yoghourt and add salt to taste. Chill and serve garnished with paprika.

Smoked mackerel dip

2 smoked mackerel fillets	1 carton *fromage blanc* (p.20)
juice of half a lemon	salt and pepper to taste
½ glass dry white wine	

Skin the mackerel fillets and pound them in a pestle and mortar or mash with a fork. Stir in the *fromage blanc* and add the lemon juice and white wine, mixing the ingredients thoroughly. Add salt and pepper to taste.

Note All these dips can be made in a liquidizer or Magimix.

Tea-leaf eggs

Tea-leaf eggs are the Chinese answer to the English pickled eggs, and are usually eaten as an hors-d'oeuvre. The eggs are boiled, soaked in a mixture of soya sauce and star-anise (page 17) and emerge marked like smooth Italian marble.

6 eggs	5 teaspoons soya sauce
1 whole star-anise	water
2 tea bags	1 dessertspoon salt

Hard-boil the eggs in water for 10 minutes. When they are cooked, remove from the heat and place under a running cold tap and leave to stand in cold water until they are cool enough to handle. Take the eggs firmly in your hand and tap the shells gently with a spoon until the shells are finely cracked but not broken. Return the eggs to the pan and pour over about 375 ml

($\frac{3}{4}$ pint) of water or sufficient to cover them. Add the star-anise, tea bags, soya sauce and salt and bring to the boil. Cover and simmer for about $2\frac{1}{2}$ hours, adding more water as required to prevent the eggs from burning in the pan. Remove from the heat and leave to stand steeped in the liquid in a cool place for about 8 hours. Just before serving, peel the eggs, cut into halves and arrange on a bed of chopped lettuce.

Eggah

The eggah originates from the Middle East and is a cross between an omelette and a quiche without pastry. The mainstay of most Middle Eastern kitchens, the beauty of it is its simplicity and versatility. You can make a plain eggah or use any filling – fish, meat, vegetables, herbs – it is an ideal way of using up left-overs. It can also be eaten hot or cold rather like a Spanish omelette. To make an eggah take one egg per person and break it into a bowl, season with salt and pepper and whisk thoroughly. Add the filling of your choice, a good pinch of the appropriate herbs and either pour into a lightly oiled oven-proof baking dish and bake in the oven, Gas Mark 4, 350°F, 180°C, for about 1 hour until it has slightly risen or cook in a non-stick covered frying-pan over a very low flame and then brown the top under a pre-heated grill. Some suggested fillings are:

Ratatouille: page 123 1 dessertspoon of ratatouille for every egg used.

Asparagus and cottage cheese: 1 small tin, 300 g ($10\frac{1}{2}$ oz), asparagus tips and 100 g (4 oz) carton of cottage cheese for four eggs.

Mint and yoghourt: 1 small carton stabilized yoghourt (page 19) and a handful of chopped mint leaves for every 4 eggs.

Chicken and tarragon: 25 g (1 oz) diced cooked chicken with chopped tarragon for every egg used.

Crabmeat and sherry: 25 g (1 oz) prepared crabmeat and 1 dessert-spoon dry sherry for every egg used.

Baked eggs with chicken livers

225 g (8 oz) chicken livers
6 eggs
1 small onion, finely chopped
1 clove garlic, finely chopped

pinch of tarragon
1 glass tomato juice
½ glass red wine
salt and pepper to taste

Roughly chop the chicken livers, add the red wine and salt and pepper to taste and leave to marinade while preparing the onions. Heat a little tomato juice and cook the onions and garlic, stirring constantly so that they do not burn or stick to the pan, adding more tomato juice as required. When the onions are quite soft add the chicken livers with the wine and stir the ingredients together. Simmer until the liver is almost cooked – brown on the outside and still pink on the inside – and remove from the heat. Spoon the livers into lightly oiled individual ramekins to form a thick layer on the bottom. Break an egg into each ramekin on top of the livers and sprinkle each with a little tarragon. Place the ramekins in a baking-dish filled with water and bake in a medium oven, Gas Mark 4, 350°F, 180°C, for about 10 minutes.

Chicken liver pâté

225 g (8 oz) chicken livers
1 medium onion, sliced
1 clove garlic, crushed
½ teaspoon mixed herbs
4-6 juniper berries, crushed

3 peppercorns
juice of 1 orange
½ glass brandy
125 ml (¼ pint) chicken stock
salt and pepper to taste

Roughly chop the chicken livers, removing any fat or gristle and place in a flat dish. Pour over the orange juice, add the mixed herbs and leave to marinade. In a heavy-based cast-iron pan heat a little stock to boiling point and cook the onions and garlic with the juniper berries and peppercorns, stirring continuously so that they do not burn or stick to the bottom of the pan. When the onions are soft, stir in the chicken livers with the orange juice and herbs. Cover and simmer for about 10 minutes – until the livers are browned outside, but slightly pink inside, adding more stock if necessary. Blend all the ingredients in a liquidizer for a smooth pâté, or if preferred mash the liver and onions with a fork for a rougher texture, and stir in the brandy. Pack the pâté into an earthenware jar, cover the top with a piece of greaseproof paper and leave to cool for a few hours before serving.

Note The pâté improves on keeping and can be made 1 or 2 days in advance.

Spinach and veal pâté

Spinach is a clean-tasting vegetable and delicious when combined with meat in a pâté or with fish as in the next recipe. To cook, wash it thoroughly and discard any of the large stringy stalks. Put in a saucepan with just enough water to prevent it from sticking to the bottom, cover and simmer over a gentle heat until it is reduced to a dark green pulp. It must be thoroughly drained and squeezed quite dry before adding to the other ingredients, otherwise the pâté will be too moist and the texture will be spoilt. If you prefer frozen spinach, make sure that it is thoroughly thawed and drained before use.

450 g (1 lb) veal	½ teaspoon marjoram
450 g (1 lb) spinach	¼ teaspoon basil
3 sorrel leaves	pinch of nutmeg
¼ teaspoon rosemary	salt and pepper to taste
½ teaspoon thyme	

Trim the veal, removing all the fat and mince it coarsely. Wash and cook the spinach and sorrel and strain into a sieve. Squeeze it dry between the palms of your hands or press it against the side of the sieve with a wooden spoon. Roughly chop the leaves and mix together with all the ingredients in a large bowl. Lightly oil a loaf tin or terrine and spoon in the mixture, pressing it down firmly. Cover with a sheet of greaseproof paper and place in a baking-dish filled with water. Bake in a warm oven, Gas Mark 3, 325°F, 170°C, for about 45-60 minutes. Serve either hot or cold.

Spinach and fish pâté

The layers of spinach and fish alternating with plain fish make a subtle colour contrast. Particular care must be taken when arranging the layers that they are quite even, otherwise the effect will be spoilt.

225 g (8 oz) white fish (cod, plaice, whiting etc.)	pinch of mixed herbs
50 g (2 oz) peeled prawns	100 g (4 oz) cottage cheese
225 g (8 oz) spinach	1 egg
1 small onion, finely sliced	juice of half a lemon
1 carrot, sliced	salt and pepper to taste

Fillet and skin the fish and roughly chop. Wash and cook the spinach and strain into a sieve. Squeeze the spinach between your hands or press it against the sides of the sieve with a wooden spoon. Put the prepared fish in a blender with the onion, carrot, herbs, cottage cheese, raw egg and lemon juice and blend until quite smooth. Remove half the mixture and set aside. Add the spinach to the remainder and blend together. Lightly oil a loaf tin or terrine and put in a layer of spinach and fish mixture. Add a layer of the plain fish mixture, cover with the prawns and add a final layer of the spinach and fish. Cover the dish securely with foil and place in a baking-dish filled with water. Bake in a moderate oven, Gas Mark 4, 350°F, 180°C, for about 1 hour. To find out whether it is cooked, insert a knife into the pâté. If it comes out clean and hot the pâté is cooked. Allow to cool before unmoulding it by dipping the terrine in hot water for a few seconds.

Note If you prefer a slightly rougher texture for this pâté, either mince all the ingredients or pass them through a vegetable mouli.

White fish mousse

Cold fish mousses are particularly attractive when set in a decorative mould. New copper moulds are expensive to buy, but it is a good idea to scour junk shops or antique markets as you can sometimes find Victorian porcelain or copper moulds quite cheaply.

450 g (1 lb) white fish, (haddock, whiting, cod, etc.)	1 small onion, sliced
	bay leaf
1 bunch watercress	6 peppercorns

2 tablespoons cultured buttermilk	water
3 teaspoons powdered gelatine	salt and pepper to taste
piece lemon rind	

To prepare the mould, lightly paint the inside with oil to prevent the mousse from sticking. Use a light bland oil like almond oil so that it will not mask the flavour of the food.

Skin and fillet the fish. Wash the watercress, pick off the leaves and set aside for decoration. To make a fish stock, boil the fish bones and heads with the onion, bay leaf and peppercorns, lemon rind and about 250 ml ($\frac{1}{2}$ pint) water for about 20 minutes, and then strain. Poach the fish and watercress leaves in the strained stock for about 10 minutes until tender, and strain. Pound the fish and watercress with a pestle and mortar to form a smooth paste, adding the buttermilk, 2 tablespoons of fish stock and salt and pepper to taste. Soften the gelatine in 3 tablespoons of water and stir into the fish. Spoon the mixture into the prepared mould and leave to set in a cool place. To unmould, dip the mould into a basin of tepid water and loosen the edges with a sharp knife. Turn the mould upside down on a wet plate and shake until the mousse works free. If the plate is wet the mousse can easily be moved on the plate without sticking. Serve garnished with small bunches of watercress leaves.

Prawn and mushroom cocktail

This recipe is a pleasant combination of flavours and makes a welcome change from the usual prawn cocktail.

500 ml (1 pint) shelled prawns	freshly chopped parsley
225 g (8 oz) button mushrooms	1 teaspoon coriander seeds,
1 lettuce heart	crushed
1 bay leaf	$\frac{1}{2}$ glass white wine
Garnish:	juice of 1 lemon
4-6 unshelled prawns	salt and pepper to taste

Sprinkle the whole mushrooms with a little salt and the crushed coriander seeds and leave to stand for about 10 minutes. Cook gently for about 3 minutes in a dry saucepan, shaking them as they give off moisture to prevent them from burning or sticking to the pan. Add the lemon juice, white wine, and the bay leaf, and simmer for a few minutes more. Remove from the heat and leave to cool. Mix the prawns with the mushrooms and marinade them for about 4 to 6 hours in the fridge. Serve on lettuce leaves, in glass dishes, garnished with a whole prawn and plenty of freshly chopped parsley.

Note If small button mushrooms are unavailable, cut the large mushrooms into quarters before cooking.

Smoked salmon cheese

This recipe is not quite as extravagant as it might at first appear. Most good delicatessen who slice their smoked salmon – as opposed to selling it pre-packed in packets – will sell the off-cuts and trimmings for about a quarter of the normal price. The trimmings are ideal for mousses and dips and only need to be carefully chopped, with any of the bones or extra fatty pieces discarded.

100 g (4 oz) smoked salmon trimmings
225 g (8 oz) cottage cheese, *or*
   fromage blanc (p.20)

1 tablespoon cultured buttermilk
juice of half a lemon
cayenne pepper

Cut the smoked salmon with a sharp knife into very small pieces. Sieve the cottage cheese or *fromage blanc* into a bowl and stir in the smoked salmon, buttermilk and lemon juice. Mix the ingredients together and add the cayenne pepper according to taste. Tightly pack into a jar and leave in the fridge for about 2 to 3 hours before serving.

Alternatively, to make a really smooth paste, blend all the ingredients together in a liquidizer or Magimix.

Mussels in orange and brandy sauce

A word of advice – always eat the mussels the same day they are bought, and if you prepare them properly you will avoid any trouble or possible poisoning.

1½ litres (3 pints) mussels
1 onion, finely chopped
1 bouquet garni
½ glass white wine
water

Sauce:
2 eggs yolks
juice and grated rind 1 orange
½ glass brandy
dash of lemon juice

To prepare the mussels, scrape with a sharp knife, under a running cold tap, to remove the beards and barnacles. Throw away any mussels with broken shells or which will not shut when the shell is tapped with a knife. Soak in cold water. In a large pan heat a little water flavoured with the onion, bouquet garni and wine until it is steaming. Put in the mussels, cover and cook over a low heat for about 5 to 7 minutes, by this time the mussels should be opened. Strain them into a colander – discarding any unopened shells – and save the liquid for the sauce. Strain the liquid through a muslin-lined sieve to get rid of any grit or sand and boil it vigorously to reduce it to half its quantity. Prepare an egg sauce in the usual way (see page 133), using the mussel liquor instead of stock. As it starts to set, whisk in the orange juice and brandy and allow to cool. If the sauce should separate, remove from the heat, and stir in a little pounded cottage cheese. Shell the mussels and arrange on a bed of chopped lettuce, pour over the sauce and garnish with the grated orange peel.

The main course

Fish, poultry, game and meat can all be served as a main course. They can be cooked in a variety of ways; baked in foil or in a brick, *en papillote*, roasted, steamed, braised and grilled and I have included recipes for all these methods.

In the case of a plainly grilled or roasted piece of fish or meat, it can be served with a sauce cooked separately. I recommend the sauce recipes on page 133 and pages 128-30 as they make a delicious accompaniment.

Fish

There seems to have been a lot of ignorance and prejudice in the past about fish. Despite the fact that Brillat-Savarin, the eminent French philosopher of food, wrote that 'it provides our tables with a most agreeable variety of dishes . . . in the hands of a skilful cook . . . [fish] can become an inexhaustible source of gustatory delight; whether it is served up whole, chopped up or in slices, boiled, fried in oil, hot or cold, it is always well received', he did not think it worthy of being served as a main course. It was rather, an entreé, a 'mezzo termine, which suits almost every temperament and may be allowed even to convalescents'. (Perhaps a little surprisingly as he also wrote that it had 'a powerful effect on the sense of physical desire and arouses the instinct of reproduction in both sexes'. Not altogether suitable for the sickroom!) Brillat-Savarin enforced the spurious argument that man needs his red meat every day by observing that 'peoples who live almost entirely on fish are less courageous than flesh eating races'. Mrs Beeton concurred and stated in the *Book of Household Management* that 'as an article of nourishment, fish is less satisfying and less stimulating than butcher's meat'. This idea, based on pure prejudice, still persists today, in spite of nutritional research which has shown the case to be otherwise.

Fish is full of goodness, and taste. It makes a satisfying meal, yet few people will serve fish as a main course even though there is a vast choice, an abundance of flavours and textures and pound for pound it is, in most cases, as cheap if not cheaper than meat. Perhaps not enough is done to encourage us to eat more fish. The White Fish Authority lists more than fifty species swimming around our shores. It seems a shame not to try them all at least once, but how many of them can we actually name or do we ever see in the shops?

During the last few years there has been a sharp increase in the frozen fish trade, but this has been at the expense of the wet fish, another example of convenience foods replacing traditional methods with the ensuing loss of standards. It is a sad fact that within the last twenty-five years, 50 per cent of all fishmongers have shut down. The days of scrubbed marble slabs covered with glinting fish piled on blocks of ice may soon be a memory of the past.

My fishmonger has a thriving business, no doubt because he offers an amazing choice of interesting and reasonably priced fish; customers come from all over London to buy from him. Over the years with boundless patience and the odd lewd remark he has broken down my prejudices, encouraged me to experiment and taught me how to buy wisely. His advice when choosing fish is to look for rigid firm flesh, bright eyes and red gills. If the fish is floppy, smells strongly and the eyes are sunken and glazed, it is obviously not fresh. A good fishmonger will not risk his reputation by selling stale fish but if it should happen inadvertently – complain. Once you have found a good fishmonger, stay with him. If his range is restricted, try and persuade him to buy a little more adventurously. He will gut, clean, scale and fillet your fish; but remember to ask for the head, bones and trimmings, you will need them for a fish stock.

Fish, high in protein and low in fat content, is a healthy, nourishing food and particularly suitable for fat-free cooking. There are many ways of cooking it: steaming, boiling, baking in foil or in a brick, grilling or poaching in a *court bouillon*. The recipes in the following chapter cover all these methods.

Court bouillon

A useful general purpose recipe for a *court bouillon* is as follows:

1 carrot, sliced	6-8 peppercorns
1 leek, sliced	1 tablespoon vinegar
1 onion, stuck with a clove	1 glass dry white wine
1 bay leaf	750 ml (1½ pints) water
1 bouquet garni	salt to taste

Put all the ingredients in a pan. Bring to the boil, cover and simmer for about 20-25 minutes. Allow to cool and strain before use.

Variations are possible, a slice of lemon or a teaspoon of pickling spices can change the flavour – see the recipe for Pickled Mackerel (page 63).

Fish needs surprisingly little cooking time. The flesh should be firm but moist and should come away from the bone when touched. Once you get in the habit of cooking and eating fish, you will be surprised that you could have ever managed without it.

Turbot in salt

Various countries have a tradition of baking a whole fish which has either been soaked, stuffed or covered in salt. I particularly like this simple Spanish recipe where the salt acts like a layer of clay under which the fish gently bakes in all its juices. The salt forms a solid crust which really does need a hammer and strong knife to break it up. It can be used again, as after baking, the salt acquires a subtle fish flavour which does well in certain soups and salads. It is preferable to use either sea or rock salt crystals for this recipe.

1 turbot
water
sufficient salt to cover

Trim and clean the fish but do not remove the skin. Place the fish in a baking-dish which is just big enough for the fish to lie flat. Cover with the salt, smoothing it down with your hands and adding the water to moisten it. Continue until the fish is completely covered with salt and sprinkle the top with water. Bake in a hot oven, Gas Mark 7, 425°F, 220°C, for about 35 minutes for a normal sized fish and remove. Leave it to cool slightly before attempting to chisel away at the salt. Once the top has been broken up, the rest will come away with the final layer. Serve either hot or cold with egg and lemon sauce (page 133).

Baked bream

Now that both salmon and sea bass are so exorbitantly expensive, I often cook a large bream instead. There is something very satisfying about its coarse full-flavoured flesh and I think it is well matched with the spiciness of coriander seeds.

1 bream, 750 g-1 kg (1½-2 lb)
1 onion, finely chopped
2 cloves garlic
1 teaspoon coriander seeds

6 peppercorns
1 teaspoon salt crystals
grated rind and juice of 1 lemon
1 carton stabilized yoghourt (p.19)

Prepare the fish brick by soaking it in water for 15 minutes. Clean and gut the bream, making sure that all its scales are removed. Crush the coriander seeds and garlic with the peppercorns and salt crystals and mix the paste with the onions and grated lemon rind. Lay the fish in a prepared fish brick and spread the mixture on, all over the fish. Pour over the lemon juice. Place the brick in a cool oven and bake for 1 hour at Gas Mark 4, 350°F, 180°C. When the fish is cooked lift it out of the brick on to a serving-dish and keep warm. Pour the juice into the yoghourt. Stir vigorously. Heat gently until almost boiling. Pour over the fish and serve immediately.

Bream with apples and horseradish

Based on a Russian recipe, the horseradish and apple sauce give the bream a pungent flavour. Fresh horseradish can sometimes be bought from a greengrocer's or at certain oriental shops, otherwise use a dried horseradish which should be soaked in lemon juice beforehand.

1 bream, 1 kg (2 lb)
2 cooking apples
2 medium onions
2 celery stalks
1 leek
2 tablespoons grated horseradish

1 bay leaf
pinch of mixed herbs
1 teaspoon honey
250 ml (½ pint) vinegar
salt and pepper

Clean and scale the fish and cut into small strips. Place the fish in a saucepan with enough vinegar to cover and bring to the boil. Remove from the heat and drain the bream, setting aside the vinegar. Meanwhile, prepare the onions, celery and leek by cutting into thin slices. Heat a little salted water (or fish stock) with a bay leaf and a pinch of mixed herbs and add the vegetables and the bream. Poach for about 5 minutes or until tender.

To prepare the sauce, peel and grate the apples and horseradish and mix with the honey, melted in a tablespoon of water and enough of the fish-flavoured vinegar to make a smooth paste.

Drain the fish and serve on a bed of the vegetables, covered with the sauce.

Sashimi – Japanese raw fish

As Peter and Joan Martin so rightly point out in their detailed book *Japanese Cooking*, there is a lot of prejudice about eating raw fish. It is actually no different from eating steak tartare or a dozen oysters but somehow few people have been convinced. The only stipulation is that only the best part of the freshest of prime fish will do and this does tend to make the dish rather expensive. But I think it really should be tried at least once. Here is their recipe.

450 g (1 lb) raw fish (sea bream, tuna, sole, smelt, cuttlefish, turbot, halibut, abalone, trout, etc.)
225 g (8 oz) Japanese radish, (daikon)

1 bunch watercress or other garnish
2 tablespoons Japanese horseradish (wasabi)
250 ml (½ pint) light soya sauce

Clean the fish carefully, removing all the bones and skin. Put the fish fillets into a colander, pour boiling water over them and immediately immerse in cold water. (The object of this exercise is not to cook the fish in any way, but simple to give some protection against surface bacteria.) There are various ways of cutting the flesh of the fish. It is usually sliced into pieces 1½ inches long, 1 inch wide and ¼ inch thick, but it can also be cut into cubes or wafers, a shape favoured for small, delicate fish such as smelt or trout. Grate the radish on a grater with large holes. Sashimi is always served in individual bowls and great care is taken that the colour and the shape of the container enhances the appearance of the fish. Put a mound of 2 or 3 tablespoons of the grated radish into each bowl and on one side of the mound arrange attractively 6-8 slices of the fish. Garnish with a sprig of watercress, other greenery or a tiny flower. Mix the horseradish with a little water to make a paste of a mustard-like consistency and put a teaspoon-ful in each bowl beside the fish. Give each guest a separate, shallow sauce bowl containing two tablespoonfuls of light soya sauce. Each guest mixes as much of the horseradish as he likes into his soya sauce, then picks up a piece of fish with chopsticks and dips it into the sauce before eating it.

Variations of the basic soya sauce which are occasionally used are as follows:

1 125 ml (¼ pint) soya sauce, 1 tablespoon grated ginger root.
2 125 ml (¼ pint) soya sauce, 1 tablespoon hot mustard.
3 125 ml (¼ pint) soya sauce, 2 tablespoons lemon juice.
4 125 ml (¼ pint) soya sauce, 2 tablespoons dried bonito flakes simmered and strained.

Plaice with orange

Traditionally, Seville oranges – the bitter marmalade oranges – were cooked with fish to give the flavour a slight edge. As their season is so short, ordinary sweet oranges sharpened with lemon juice makes an acceptable alternative.

4 plaice
2 medium onions, finely sliced
1 leek, sliced
½ teaspoon paprika
1 teaspoon mint, chopped
1 bay leaf

3 peppercorns
juice and grated rind of 3 Seville oranges, or 2 sweet oranges and 1 lemon
250 ml (½ pint) water
salt and pepper to taste

Wash, gut and fillet the fish. Lay it on a flat plate, season with salt and pepper, pour over the orange juice, cover with the mint and leave to marinade. Cook the fish trimmings with one of the onions, leek, bay leaf, peppercorns and water to make a stock. Strain and heat a small amount in a saucepan until bubbling. Stir in the paprika and cook over a fierce heat, stirring continuously for a few seconds. Add more stock, the rest of the onions and the grated orange rind, and cook until the onions are soft. Adjust the seasoning and spoon the mixture over the fish. Balance the plate of fish over a saucepan filled with boiling water and steam the fish until tender (about 20 minutes). Serve immediately.

Fisch-gulasch

The Austrians eat mainly fresh-water fish – for obvious reasons –
and they tend to season it rather highly. I have adapted the recipe
to our sea-water fish.

675 g (1½ lb) fish (whiting, cod, skate, rock salmon etc.)	1 bay leaf
	8 peppercorns
6 onions, sliced	1 carton stabilized yoghourt (p.19)
1 leek, sliced	water
1½ tablespoons paprika	salt and pepper to taste

Wash, gut and fillet the fish. Cut into small strips about 2 inches
long and sprinkle with paprika. Cook the fish trimmings with one
of the onions, leek, bay leaf, peppercorns and enough water to
make about 375 ml (¾ pint) fish stock. Strain and heat a small
amount in a saucepan. Add the rest of the onions and cook until
soft. Add the fish and cook for a minute in the dry heat before
stirring in the remainder of the stock. Cover and simmer for
about half an hour. When the fish is tender, add the yoghourt and
simmer, stirring continuously for a few minutes before serving.

Trout in wine

An unusual variation of this recipe is to use a mixture of wines. I
once read that a combination of four parts white wine to one part
of Madeira and one part of white rum made an excellent *court
bouillon,* and it is delicious, if rather extravagant!

I often poach trout in an excellent rice wine which friends of
mine make in Wales and are kind enough to give me a bottle of on
their occasional visits to London, or in a mixture of unsweetened
natural apple juice and cheap dry French wine. Whatever wines
you use, do watch out that they are not oversweet, as the taste
will mask that of the fish. Adjustments can always be made after
cooking by the addition of a dash of fresh lemon juice or wine
vinegar, so that the dish will not be totally ruined.

6 trout weighing 160-225 g (6-8 oz) each

1 onion, sliced

1 carrot, sliced

375 ml (¾ pint) wine mixture made from dry white wine, cider, dry sherry, rice wine, extra dry vermouth, etc.

1 celery stalk, sliced

1 bay leaf

½ teaspoon thyme

6 peppercorns

1 tablespoon wine vinegar

salt to taste

6 lemon slices

Simmer all the ingredients together, except the trout, for about 15 minutes, to make a good *court bouillon*. Lay the trout in a flat pan and pour over the liquid. Either bake the fish in a slow oven, Gas Mark 2, 300°F, 150°C, basting occasionally, or simmer over a low heat until tender. Remove the fish and skin and fillet them, and arrange in a dish. Return the skin, heads and bones to the pan with the cooking liquid and boil vigorously until it has reduced to half its quantity. Strain and pour over the fish. Serve either hot or cold decorated with lemon slices. If left to cool, the liquid will set after a few hours to a clear pale jelly, and the dish served chilled is ideal for a summer buffet.

Honeyed trout

The Moors, who conquered Southern Spain in the Middle Ages, had a very distinctive sense of taste. They combined sweet with savoury; meat cooked with honey, cinnamon and raisins is a well-known example. This dish shows how strong their influence was, as it has survived centuries of peasant cooking and is accepted as truly Spanish in its origin. Incidentally, English cooking is not without its contrasts in taste – what about firm favourites like pork chops with apple sauce, or lamb served with apricots (pages 111 and 105)?

6 trout weighing 160-225 g (6-8 oz) each

2 medium onions, sliced

100 g (4 oz) mushrooms

1 teaspoon ground cumin

2 tablespoons honey

1 glass dry white wine

2 tablespoons fish stock or water

salt and pepper to taste

Prepare the fish brick if necessary by soaking it in water for 15 minutes. Gut and clean the fish. Place the fish in a shallow dish and cover with the onions, mushrooms and ground cumin and salt and pepper to taste. Gently heat the honey in a saucepan with the stock or water until it has melted to form a clear liquid. Add the wine and pour over the fish. Leave the trout to marinade for about an hour in a cool place. Transfer the fish and vegetables to a prepared fish brick and cook in a fairly hot oven, Gas Mark 6, 400°F, 200°C, for about 15 minutes or bake in a covered ovenproof dish, at Gas Mark 3, 325°F, 170°C, until tender. Serve immediately.

Pickled mackerel

I like to make up my own blend of pickling spice, just because I love handling the spices. It includes coriander and mustard seeds, cassia, ginger, peppercorns, bay leaf, pimento, cloves, chillies, mace and cardamoms. I must admit to being a little haphazard about the proportions but they are roughly 3 parts of coriander and mustard seeds to 2 parts ginger, bay leaf and pimento, to 1 part of everything else. Actually, both Bart Spices and Sainsbury's make an excellent blend which would save you the trouble.

4 mackerel
1 large onion, sliced in rings
1 teaspoon pickling spice
1 dried chilli
1 bay leaf, crushed

6 peppercorns
250 ml ($\frac{1}{2}$ pint) court bouillon (p.56)
juice of 1 lemon
8 lemon slices

Clean and gut the mackerel. They can either be baked whole or skinned and filleted, in which case allow about a quarter of an hour less cooking time for the fillets. Lay the fish in a flat dish and sprinkle over the pickling spice, chilli, peppercorns and crushed bay leaf. Arrange the onion rings on top of the mackerel. Mix the lemon juice with the *court bouillon* and pour over the fish. Cover with foil and bake in a slow oven, Gas Mark 2, 300°F, 150°C, for about an hour, basting occasionally. Decorate with the lemon slices and serve either hot or cold. If the fish is left to cool the taste of the spices becomes much stronger and the liquid will set to a palish jelly.

Mackerel grilled with fennel

Mackerel are particularly suitable to grill as they are an oily fish. I like to keep their heads and tails on – it makes the fish look far more complete. Make three diagonal slashes with a sharp knife on either side of the fish before cooking. If cooking with fresh fennel either use the branches and the feathery tips of sweet fennel or the 'tuber', a whitish bulb, of the Florence fennel which is slightly sweeter in taste. Whichever fennel you use, cut into small pieces and poach in dry cider until tender. Spread the fennel on the bottom of a flat dish, place the gutted and cleaned fish on top and pour over the cider. Cook under a hot grill, allowing between 7-10 minutes each side.

South Indian steamed haddock

Adapted from a South Indian recipe, the fish should be wrapped in a whole banana leaf and then steamed. Unfortunately, banana leaves are not to be easily found in this country – perhaps a curator at Kew Gardens might oblige? Seriously, there just isn't any English leaf either large or resilient enough so I have to make do with well-oiled greaseproof paper.

1 fresh haddock weighing 1 kg (2 lb)	8-10 fresh green chillies
	500 ml (1 pint) yoghourt
1 large bunch coriander leaves *or* parsley	salt to taste

Clean and gut the fish, slit the stomach open and lay flat on a large piece of well-oiled greaseproof paper. Top and tail the green chillies and roughly chop. Tear the coriander or parsley leaves from their stalks and grind with the chillies and a little salt in a vegetable mouli or pestle and mortar to form a smooth paste. Stir in with the yoghourt and pour over the fish. Wrap the fish loosely in the greaseproof paper. Place on a rack suspended over a baking-dish half filled with water. Bake in a moderate oven, Gas Mark 4, 350°F, 180°C, for about 35-45 minutes until cooked. Unwrap on to a serving plate so that none of the juices escape.

Squid stewed in tomatoes and wine

When I lived in Morocco the family would sometimes drive out to Mohammeddia – Casablanca's fishing port – to spend a lazy day riding the surf and soaking up the glorious sun. About six o'clock, when we were packed up to go home, the fishing boats would chug into the harbour, sienna sails creased on to fish-piled decks; the boys were back and trading began. Luckily my brother-in-law spoke Arabic and he was left to cope with the serious business of fixing the price while my sister and I scrambled for the fish. The choice was incredible, shapes, sizes and colours jumbled together that sadly are too rarely seen on our marble slabs, and it was there that I saw and bought squid for the first time. Happily I can now buy it in London, although in certain shops little is done to distinguish it from its vastly inferior cousin the cuttle fish.

1 kg (2 lb) squid	1 large pinch of cinnamon
450 g (1 lb) tomatoes (peeled and chopped or 396 g (14 oz) tin)	1 glass red wine
	2 tablespoons water
1 large onion	salt and pepper to taste
1 clove garlic	chopped parsley
1 tablespoon tomato purée	

To prepare the squid, separate the head from the body. Cut the tentacles and gently pull the ink sac from the head, discarding the rest of the head. Ease the transparent backbone away from the body and squeeze out the innards. Peel off the flesh-pink skin and then wash the body and tentacles. Chop into rings and leave to drain. Mix the water with the tomato purée and heat in a saucepan. Gently cook the onion and garlic for 5 minutes and add the tomatoes and cinnamon. Crush the ink sacs through a sieve and add the juice to the pan. Stir in the red wine and squid and stew gently for about 15-20 minutes until the squid is cooked. It should be firm but not too rubbery. If the sauce is too watery, remove the squid and keep it warm and reduce the sauce until it is thick and richly flavoured. Adjust the seasoning, pour the sauce over the squid and serve sprinkled with chopped parsley.

Barbecued masala fish

Choose a large fish – bream, turbot, halibut or plaice, the English equivalent of the Indian pomfret – and cook it on an open charcoal fire. I use a small Portuguese cast-iron stove which can be set up at a moment's notice, but there are a variety of suitable barbecues available from most hardware shops or garden centres. Make sure that the charcoal is glowing, as it is the heat rather than the flames which cook the fish, and that the grid is well oiled so that the fish does not stick to it. If you do not have a barbecue, the fish can always be cooked under a preheated grill.

1 whole fish weighing 1-1½ kg (2-3 lb)	1 teaspoon ground ginger
4 cloves garlic	1 teaspoon turmeric powder
1 tablespoon garam masala	½ teaspoon cumin seeds
1 tablespoon red chilli powder	juice of ½ lemon
	salt and pepper to taste

Clean and gut the fish and make three incisions with a sharp knife on either side. With the blunt edge of a knife, crush the garlic cloves and cumin seeds with a little salt to form a paste – this can be done in a pestle and mortar if preferred – and mix in the red chilli powder, ground ginger and turmeric. Paint the mixture all over the fish, not forgetting inside the gashes and the head and leave to marinate in a cool place for a minimum of an hour. When it is ready to be cooked, pierce it lengthways with a skewer to stop it from curling up and cook over the barbecue, turning it every 4-5 minutes. Brush it occasionally with the lemon juice and sprinkle with the garam masala as you turn the fish. Depending on the fire used, it should take about 25 minutes to cook. Serve with a cooling raita (page 46).

Creamed scallops

Scallops were obviously an important food in the eighteenth and nineteenth centuries as their motif appears constantly on little objects – wooden inlaid boxes, silver ashtrays, hand-turned furniture – and even lace was intricately 'scalloped' around the border.

Sadly, they are too expensive to eat regularly – although I have noticed that around the springtime they can be bought from between 20 and 30p each, which I suppose is quite reasonable considering the present cost of living.

10-12 scallops	juice of half a lemon
100 g (4 oz) button mushrooms	1 carton *fromage blanc* (p.20)
1 glass dry white wine	pinch of cayenne pepper
125 ml (¼ pint) fish stock	salt and pepper to taste

Prepare the scallops by removing them from their shells and prising away the beard. Wash in running cold water to get rid of all the grit, and cut into thick slices and leave to drain. Salt the mushrooms and cook in a heavy pan, shaking constantly so that they do not burn or stick to the bottom of the pan. As soon as they start to release their juice, remove from the heat. Add the scallops, freshly ground black pepper and add the lemon juice, white wine and fish stock. Cover and simmer for 10 minutes or until the scallops are tender. Meanwhile, warm the *fromage blanc* in a double boiler but do not allow to boil as it will curdle. When the scallops are cooked, remove from the pan and keep warm. Whisk the mushrooms and the sauce into the *fromage blanc* and pour over the scallops. Sprinkle with cayenne pepper and serve immediately.

Chinese steamed fish

Chinese cookery has a great tradition of steaming and the firm flesh of the grey mullet acquires a subtle flavour when cooked in this fashion. The fish is cleaned and gutted and laid on an earthenware dish. It is rubbed all over with salt, garlic and fresh ginger and marinaded in a mixture of two parts sherry to one of soya sauce for a few hours. The decoration is most important both for the taste and the appearance. The ingredients vary according to their availability but spring onions, dried or fresh shrimps and mushrooms, lotus roots, fresh chives, shredded ham or pork, slices of lemon, radishes and slices of Chinese cabbage are used. The whole dish is then placed in the steamer and cooked until the fish is tender – the flesh should fall away from the bones when touched with chopsticks.

It is worthwhile either buying a steamer or improvising one by balancing a plate over a saucepan filled with boiling water. Just taste this dish.

Sweet and sour fish

Sweet and sour carp is a dish eaten at Chinese festivals. It symbolizes rewards (the sweet) through endeavour (the sour), and has place of honour at a feast. Unfortunately, carp is not too easy to buy so I have adapted the delicious sauce to be served with the most English of fishes – skate.

1 kg (2 lb) skate	2 tablespoons dry sherry
1 onion	1 tablespoon soya sauce
1 clove garlic	1 teaspoon honey
1 green pepper	1 dessertspoon wine vinegar
100 g (4 oz) mushrooms	250 ml (½ pint) fish stock (p.26)
1 teaspoon paprika	salt and pepper to taste

The best method of cooking is to use a wok (see page 00). If you do not have one, an ordinary thick-based saucepan will do. It is just that it does not give such an overall heat spread and, as it will not have curved sides, the ingredients will have to be strained and removed from the pan instead of resting on the sides. Prepare the stock and leave to cool. As in all Chinese cooking, the art of preparation is as important as cooking. Clean and fillet the skate and cut into 1-inch cubes, and sprinkle with paprika. Finely slice the onion and garlic, shred the pepper and cut the mushrooms into quarters. Heat the stock with the sherry, soya sauce, honey and wine vinegar until boiling. Add the onions and garlic and spread them out so that they cook evenly. Stir in the green pepper and mushrooms and cook for about 1 minute and remove. Add the fish, cook for 4 minutes and remove from the stock. Use either a slotted metal spoon or a Chinese ladle to drain the ingredients. Return the fish and vegetables to the wok, stir, adjust the seasoning and serve immediately.

Grilled swordfish kebabs

In Spain the *pez espada* is considered a delicacy. Eaten lightly
smoked and carved into wafer-thin slices or marinaded and
grilled *à la parilla* (on an open fire) it is mouthwateringly good. Its
natural habitat is warmer waters than our surrounding seas, so
sadly it is all too rarely found on sale. I use either fresh tunny or
sunfish for this recipe; both are like swordfish, firm, meaty fish
which do not fall apart or flake while cooking and so are ideal for
kebabs.

675 g (1½ lb) swordfish, *or* fresh
   tunny, sunfish *or* rock salmon
20 bay leaves
Marinade:
1 small onion, finely chopped

2 cloves garlic
1 tablespoon cultured buttermilk
juice of half a lemon
salt and freshly ground black
   pepper

Skin and fillet the fish and cut into 1-inch cubes. Crush the clove
of garlic and a few crystals of rock salt with the blunt edge of a
knife and combine with the other ingredients of the marinade.
Place the prepared fish in a bowl, pour over the marinade and
turn the fish in it so that it is well and truly coated. Leave for a
minimum of 3 hours. If you are using fresh bay leaves these
should be added to the marinade, but dried leaves must be
soaked for an hour in boiling water until softened, drained and
then added to the fish. When the fish is ready, thread it on to a
kebab stick or skewer, alternating a cube of fish with a bay leaf.
Grill over a glowing charcoal fire or under a pre-heated grill for
about 10 minutes, turning occasionally. To prevent the fish from
drying, baste with the marinade while cooking. Serve hot with a
delicious summer salad.

Haddock soufflé

I have tried not to include any recipe in this book which calls for
the use of additional starch or carbohydrate. This is the one
honourable exception—it was too great a temptation to resist!

450 g (1 lb) fresh haddock
1 leek, sliced
1 onion, sliced
1 teaspoon tomato purée
1 bouquet garni
4-6 peppercorns
1 teaspoon cornflour

100 g (4 oz) cottage cheese
1 teaspoon Burgess anchovy
  essence
1 bay leaf
2 egg whites
375 ml (¾ pint) water

To prepare a soufflé dish, lightly oil the inside and tie a band of greaseproof paper around the outside to stand about 2 inches above the rim.

Fillet the haddock and cook the skin and bones with the onion, leek, bay leaf and water to make a stock. Strain the liquid, discarding the fish skin and bones, add the bouquet garni and peppercorns and poach the fish in the stock until tender. Remove the fish and leave to cool. Strain the stock, boil it vigorously until it has reduced to half its original quantity (about 165 ml (⅓ pint)) and mix in the teaspoon of tomato purée and anchovy essence. Simmer for a further 3-4 minutes and set aside. Liquidize the cottage cheese or pass it through a sieve. Beat the cornflour into the sauce and add the cottage cheese, whisking the whole time. If you have a liquidizer do use it, as the sauce should be as well blended as possible. Flake the haddock and use half to line the prepared soufflé dish, and stir the remainder into the sauce. Beat the egg whites until stiff and fold them into the sauce with a metal spoon. Pour the sauce over the fish and bake in a pre-heated oven, Gas Mark 5, 375° F, 190° C, for 10 to 15 minutes. Serve immediately.

Note This is the master recipe for a soufflé and can be adapted to any ingredients.

Red mullet en papillote

A truly delicious fish, red mullet is often cooked *en papillote*. The fish is scaled, gutted, rubbed with salt and garlic and wrapped in lightly oiled greaseproof paper and baked in a moderate oven, Gas Mark 5, 375° F, 190° C, for about 25 minutes.

Red mullet in tomatoes and wine

When the fish are being gutted make sure that the livers are not thrown away. Jane Grigson in her excellent book *Fish Cookery* suggests eating the liver—it was apparently a great delicacy of the Romans—and I find it gives a superb flavour to the tomato sauce.

6 red mullet
1 onion, sliced
2 cloves garlic
450 g (1 lb) fresh tomatoes
1 teapoon oregano

½ teaspoon cinnamon (optional)
125 ml (¼ pint) tomato juice
glass red wine
salt and pepper to taste
chopped parsley

Clean and gut the fish and remove the livers. Arrange the fish in a shallow baking dish. Heat the tomato juice gently and in it cook the onion and garlic. Peel and chop the tomatoes and add to the pan. Add the oregano, red wine, salt and pepper and the cinnamon if you prefer a sweet, more Mediterranean flavoured sauce. Leave the sauce to simmer until it starts to reduce to a thickish purée. Chop the livers and stir into the pan. Cook for 3-4 minutes and then remove from the heat. Spoon the sauce over the fish and bake covered, in a moderate oven, Gas Mark 4, 350° F, 180° C, for 25 minutes, or simmer on top of the stove in a large casserole. Serve sprinkled with freshly chopped parsley.

Chicken

When I was a child, my parents used to take the family out for the occasional Sunday lunch. We always used to go to the same restaurant hidden away by the River Thames and we always chose the same meal—Chicken in a Basket with Barbecue Sauce. The joys of hot spicy chicken eaten with the fingers with a huge starched napkin tucked around the neck in a vain attempt to keep one's clothes clean, never fail to evoke fond memories.

Chicken in those days—and it was only twenty-five years ago—was considered a luxury. Joints of roast beef or leg of lamb were a regular occurrence for a Sunday lunch and chicken was reserved for a special treat. Nowadays the opposite is true; few of us can afford to have a joint of meat, whereas intensive poultry-farming methods have brought chicken within the reach of most of our purses. Sadly, quality has been compromised for quantity. Battery-reared birds are on the whole rather tasteless. Fed on meal prepared from a large proportion of ground fish-bones, which are no doubt nourishing and high in protein, they end up tasting more of fish than meat.

Understandably, I prefer to buy a free-range fresh bird either from my fishmonger or from a stall at the local market where the quality is excellent and the prices reasonable. It is worth the effort to search out a good source of fresh, tender chicken as it makes all the difference in terms of flavour. If you do use a frozen bird, make sure that it is completely thawed and wiped dry before cooking, otherwise it will end up being tasteless (and a possible source of infection).

Chicken is very versatile. It has a low fat content and is easy and economical to cook. Depending on what I intend to cook, I either choose a roasting or boiling fowl, but as a general rule I use a boiler if I want to make a cold dish as the meat is more succulent. A boiler is good value pound per pound and there is the added bonus of the cooking liquid which after it has been skimmed, makes a delicious stock and can be used as the base for sauces and soups. To cook a boiling fowl, I slowly simmer it in enough water to cover, with an onion cut in quarters, a chopped carrot, a bouquet garni, and a bay leaf, a few peppercorns, a pinch of salt and any other vegetables which I might happen to have handy like leeks, celery, tomatoes or courgettes. It should be left to stand in the broth for about half an hour after it is cooked and then drained, skinned and carved. I have included a recipe for a chicken soufflé (page 78), but it goes well also with any variation of the egg sauce (page 133) or ratatouille (page 123). There are various ways to cook a roaster. I find my meat brick invaluable but a heavy casserole made of cast-iron or good pottery is useful. The chicken is placed in the prepared brick or casserole and then tightly covered so that none of the juices escapes. The lid can be removed for the last 10 minutes of cooking time to allow the skin to crisp or brown. I personally never use a 'cooking bag' as I think they are a waste of time. I find tin foil works just as well and is a lot cheaper. The foil should be lightly oiled to prevent it from sticking and then wrapped around the chicken and placed in a baking-tray. It is completely unnecessary to add any extra fat to a chicken or meat while cooking. It will not dry out if it is well covered and able to absorb its own juices, and it makes for a much cleaner flavour. Chicken can be steamed (page 77) or grilled. Marinade the portions in some lemon juice, a pinch of thyme or oregano and some freshly ground pepper and then place under a pre-heated grill, turning occasionally until cooked.

I also like to stuff a chicken both in the cavity and between the skin and flesh so that the flavour can seep through and the breast stays really moist. My first two recipes are for chicken stuffed with aubergines and chicken stuffed with herbs. The possibilities with chicken are endless—it is adaptable and lends itself to a variety of tastes and flavours. I have selected a few well-tried and firm favourites, but I do advise you to experiment for yourself.

Stuffed aubergine and cumin chicken

1 chicken 1-1½ kg (2½-3½ lb)
2 large aubergines

1 dessertspoon cumin powder
salt and pepper to taste

Prepare the meat brick by soaking it in water for 15 minutes.

Wipe the chicken and work the skin free by sliding your fingers over the breast under the skin, pulling it loose but taking care not to tear it.

Thinly slice the aubergines, sprinkle with salt and leave to stand for about an hour so that the bitterness drains out. When they have sweated sufficiently, rinse and pat dry, season and sprinkle them with cumin, leaving a little to rub into the skin of the chicken. Slide in the slices of aubergine over the breast, patting so that they spread evenly all over. Stuff the cavity as full as possible. Place the chicken in a prepared brick, covering it with any left-over slices of aubergine, sprinkle over the remaining cumin and bake in a pre-heated oven, Gas Mark 8, 450° F, 230° C, for about 1-1¼ hours. If you want to crisp the skin, remove the top of the chicken brick about 10 minutes before it is cooked to allow the skin to brown.

Stuffed herb chicken

Do try to use fresh herbs for this recipe as I cannot tell you what a difference it makes to the flavour. If you do not have them at hand, use dried herbs and as many as you like. You really cannot overdo the quantities for this recipe.

1 chicken weighing 1-1½ kg (2½-3½ lb)
1 clove garlic, crushed
1 tablespoon parsley, chopped
1 tablespoon chives, chopped
1 tablespoon tarragon, chopped
1 tablespoon rosemary, chopped
1 tablespoon oregano, chopped

1 tablespoon thyme, chopped
1 tablespoon summer savory, chopped
1 small carton cottage cheese
½ glass dry white wine
250 ml (½ pint) chicken stock
salt and pepper

Prepare the meat brick by soaking it in water for 15 minutes. Wipe the chicken with a damp cloth and loosen the skin as directed in the previous recipe. Sieve the cottage cheese into a large bowl and mix in all the herbs with the garlic and the white wine until it has formed a smooth paste. Spoon the mixture on to the breast of the chicken, under the skin, and pat it until it is spread evenly. Tie up the chicken and put it in the prepared brick. Roast in a hot oven, Gas Mark 8, 450° F, 230° C, until it is cooked, about 1-1½ hours. Remove the brick, keeping it warm. To make a gravy, strain the juices from the brick into a saucepan and add the chicken stock. Bring to the boil and cook vigorously until the quantity has reduced by about one-third. Adjust the seasoning, sprinkle with freshly chopped parsley and serve with the chicken.

Roast chicken with dried fruit stuffing

This is a Persian dish which combines the sweet and savoury tastes and is often served at feasts and festivals to symbolize the contrast of life.

1 chicken weighing 1-1¼ kg (2½-3 lb)
1 medium onion, finely chopped
160 g (6 oz) dried apricots
100 g (4 oz) prunes
50 g (2 oz) raisins

pinch of cinnamon
juice of half a lemon
salt and pepper to taste
125 ml (¼ pint) chicken stock

Wash the dried fruit in cold water and soak overnight in a solution of cold weak tea to give the fruit extra flavour. Drain and roughly chop, removing any stones. Prepare the meat brick, if you are going to use it, by soaking it in water for 15 minutes. Heat the stock and cook the onion until soft. Stir in the fruit and add the cinnamon and lemon juice. Simmer for about 10 minutes and adjust the seasoning. Stuff the inside of the chicken with the fruit and rub the skin with the lemon skin. Cook in a moderate oven either wrapped in foil or in a prepared brick for about an hour on Gas Mark 8, 450° F, 230° C.

Poulet poché romaine

The Grill Room at the Dorchester Hotel was one of the first restaurants to include a choice of 'fat-free' dishes in their menu. Oeuf en Cocotte au Fromage Blanc, Filet de Turbot Poché aux Algues, and Cuisse de Volaille à la Sauge to name but a few. Anton Mosimann, their Maitre Chef de Cuisine, was the innovator and he has created especially for this book a new recipe which is quite delicious.

1 chicken weighing 1½ kg (3½ lb)
1 small onion, sliced
¼ teaspoon ground cloves
1 bay leaf
1 piece lemon rind
6 peppercorns
1½ litres (3 pints) chicken stock
salt to taste

Sauce:
2 celery stalks, sliced
1 green pepper, sliced
2 carrots, sliced
100 g (4 oz) mushrooms, chopped
1 teaspoon fennel seeds
2 teaspoons Worcestershire sauce
juice of half a lemon
500 ml (1 pint) tomato juice
salt and pepper to taste
chopped parsley

Wipe the chicken with a damp cloth. Place it in a saucepan with the onion, cloves, bay leaf, lemon rind, peppercorns and salt, and add the stock. Poach the chicken for about 20 minutes and remove from the heat. Leave it to cool in the liquid so that it cooks gently as it cools. To prepare the sauce, heat the tomato juice with all the remaining ingredients and simmer until the vegetables are tender. Liquidize the sauce or pass through a sieve to make a purée. Joint the chicken and remove the skin with a sharp knife. Arrange on a dish and pour the sauce over it. Serve garnished with chopped parsley.

Chicken and cider

Chicken and cider is an unusual but thoroughly successful combination. What cider and apples you use will depend on how sweet you like the dish. I admit to rather a sweet tooth so I use a medium dry cider and a firm eater like Winter Pearman, but if your taste is slightly sharper, I would suggest using a dry cider and a Bramley or some other cooking apple.

1 chicken weighing 1-1½ kg
    (2½-3½ lb)
2 leeks, finely sliced
2 carrots, finely sliced
2 tomatoes, peeled
pinch of cinnamon
1 large glass cider (see note below)
salt and pepper

Stuffing:
1 chicken liver, about 50 g (2 oz)
100 g (4 oz) veal
1 leek, finely chopped
1 tomato, peeled and chopped
1 apple, peeled and grated
1 teaspoon mixed herbs
½ teaspoon marjoram
½ teaspoon parsley
1 egg
salt and pepper to taste

Prepare the meat brick, if you are going to use it, by soaking in water for 15 minutes. Clean and wipe the chicken and rub it all over with salt, pepper and cinnamon. To prepare the stuffing, mince the veal and chicken liver together and mix with the leek, tomato, apple, egg and herbs. I find that the easiest way is to put all the ingredients in a Magimix or blender and give it a short, sharp whirl. If you do not have one then I am afraid there is no easy way out—you will have to do it all by hand. Stuff the chicken and place it in the prepared brick with the chopped vegetables and pour on the cider. Bake covered in a medium oven, Gas Mark 5, 375° F, 190° C, for about 1 hour. Remove the chicken and carve into portions. Skim and liquidize the gravy or pass through a sieve, reducing the vegetables to a purée.

Note If you are cooking this dish in an ordinary casserole you may have to increase the quantity of cider to prevent the chicken drying out.

Steamed chicken breasts with courgettes

Steaming 'is a process of cookery which is particularly adapted to very delicate preparations. When any delicate preparation is to be steamed, the cook should on no account boil anything strong and highly flavoured in the vessel under it. For instance, liquor containing vegetables must not be boiled under a pudding, or the flavour of the latter will be entirely spoilt.' (Anon) Straightforward instructions which are as relevant today as they were when written in 1840.

4 chicken breasts	juice of 1 lemon
450 g (1 lb) courgettes	salt and pepper to taste
1 teaspoon tarragon	

Remove the skin from the chicken breasts and with a sharp knife make small incisions all over. Lay them in a flat dish and pour over the lemon juice, a little salt and freshly ground black pepper. Leave to marinade for a minimum of 1 hour. Wash and chop the courgettes into 1-inch slices and dry thoroughly. Place the courgettes on the bottom of the steamer and sprinkle with the tarragon, arrange the chicken breasts on top and finish off with another layer of tarragon. Steam gently for about 20 minutes until cooked.

Note If you do not have a steamer, use an ordinary plate suspended over a saucepan half filled with water.

Cold chicken soufflé

Mrs A B Marshall's *Larger Cookery Book of Extra Recipes,* is a storehouse of beautiful illustrations in the Victorian tradition and amazingly good fancy recipes. Her presentation was impeccable – each dish had to be meticouloulsy decorated and her little Soufflés of Chicken Cold (*sic*) were perfection. I have adapted the recipe slightly, substituting egg sauce for cream, and I suggest that rather than making your own aspic you use a packet of Symington's which is widely available.

225 g (8 oz) cold cooked chicken
1 teaspoon tarragon, chopped
1 teaspoon chervil, chopped
1 teaspoon parsley, chopped
250 ml (½ pint) cold egg sauce
  (p.133)

100 g (4 oz) cottage cheese
500 ml (1 pint) aspic
1 dessertspoon tarragon vinegar
pinch of cayenne pepper
salt and pepper to taste

Garnish: 1 slice of cooked ham or tongue, sprigs of chervil, 1 teaspoon chopped parsley.

To prepare the soufflé dish, lightly oil the inside and tie a band of greaseproof paper around the outside, to stand about 2 inches above the rim. Prepare the aspic according to the directions on the packet and leave to cool until almost set. Chop the chicken finely, discarding the skin and sinew, and mix in a bowl with the egg sauce, the sieved or pounded cottage cheese, vinegar, herbs and cayenne pepper. Adjust the seasoning. Fold the aspic into the mixture and stir all the ingredients together. Spoon into the prepared soufflé dish and leave to set in a cool place. Decorate the soufflé with cut-out diamond shapes of cooked ham or tongue, sprigs of chervil and chopped parsley, remove the greaseproof band and serve.

Chicken turmeric

This Middle Eastern dish is a useful way of cooking chicken joints
or portions. The delicate slightly peppery taste of turmeric
permeates the meat and colours it an attractive soft yellow.

4 chicken joints or portions
½ teaspoon turmeric powder
1 cardamom pod, crushed
juice of half a lemon

125 ml (¼ pint) chicken stock
water
salt and pepper to taste
chopped parsley

Heat the stock in a heavy-based enamelled casserole. When it is
bubbling, stir in the turmeric powder, the cardamom pod, lemon
juice and enough water to prevent the powder from burning and
turning brown. Slowly bring to the boil and add the chicken
joints. Season with salt and plenty of freshly ground black
pepper, cover and simmer for about half an hour or until the meat
is cooked. It will need watching as the chicken should be turned
frequently, and as it absorbs the juices more water should be
added, a little at a time. Serve hot, garnished with freshly
chopped parsley.

Chicken curry

Spices were originally used in Indian cooking for their medicinal
and preservative properties as well as for their flavour. The
Indian system of medicine, *Ayurveda* or The Science of Life, is very
specific about the use of spices in cooking. They were attributed
curative properties and were eaten to help maintain the good
health of the body.

1 chicken weighing 1-1¼ kg (2½-
   3 lb)
2 onions, finely chopped
2 cloves garlic
1 piece root ginger, peeled
1 teaspoon turmeric

1 small tin, 226 g (8 oz) tomatoes
1 carton stabilized yoghourt (p.20)
1 fresh green chilli
salt and pepper to taste

Cut the chicken into portions and with a sharp knife remove the
skin. Either in a pestle and mortar or with a sharp knife crush the
garlic, green chilli and ginger with a little salt to make a smooth

paste. Strain the tomatoes and heat a little juice in a thick-based enamelled pan. Add the onions and cook for a few minutes. Stir in the garlic paste with the turmeric and a little more tomato juice if the mixture is too dry. The important thing is that while the spices need heat in order to release their flavour, they must not be allowed to burn or dry up as it will completely spoil the taste. Stir constantly and allow the spices to bubble for a few minutes. Add the chicken joints, turning them so that they brown on all sides. Add the tomatoes, cover and simmer until the meat is tender, stirring occasionally and adding more tomato juice as required. Just before serving adjust the seasoning and add the yoghourt.

Tandoori chicken

Most Indian restaurants serve a dish which is no more than a pale imitation of Tandoori chicken. The chicken should be steeped in a subtle blend of spices and marinaded for a minimum of 5 hours – something that rarely happens. To do it properly the chicken should be baked in a clay-lined oven or tandoori, but a spit roaster or suspending it with hooks in an ordinary oven will do. Red colouring should be rubbed all over the bird for a final authentic touch.

1 chicken weighing 1¼-2 kg (3-4 lb)	juice of 2 lemons
2 cloves garlic	3-4 drops cochineal
2 teaspoons chilli powder	1 carton low-fat yoghourt
1 teaspoon ground ginger	salt and freshly ground black
1 teaspoon coriander powder	pepper to taste
1 teaspoon cumin powder	

Clean and wipe the chicken dry and remove the skin with a sharp knife. Rub it all over with the used lemon skins, sprinkle with salt and leave for half an hour. Crush the garlic cloves with a little salt and mix with all the spices, the yoghourt, lemon juice and plenty of freshly ground black pepper. Paint the marinade both inside and outside the chicken – I find a pastry brush invaluable for this – and leave to marinade in a cool place for a minimum of 5 hours. Pre-heat the spit roaster, skewer the chicken and cook for half an hour. For an ordinary oven, pre-heat to Gas Mark 8, 450°F,

230°C, and either put the chicken directly on the middle oven shelf with a tray on the lower shelf to catch the drips or suspend it from the top shelf skewered with S-shaped meat hooks or twisted wire hangers. Cook for half an hour, basting occasionally with the marinade.

To prepare the colouring mix the cochineal with the remaining marinade and paint all over the chicken. Return it to the oven and cook for a further 10 minutes until it is really crisp. Serve with raita (page 46) and a green salad.

Note Tandoori chicken can also be cooked on an open charcoal stove or barbecue.

Chicken breasts with fresh ginger

4 chicken breasts	5 cardamom seeds
1 large onion	1 teaspoon turmeric
2 cloves garlic	2 tablespoons soya or teryski sauce
2-inch piece root ginger	2 tablespoons dry sherry

Grate the onion, peel and finely chop the ginger and garlic and mix with the soya sauce in a large bowl. Boil the sherry in a small saucepan until it is reduced by half and the alcohol has evaporated, and stir into the marinade with the turmeric. Place the chicken breasts in the marinade and sprinkle with the cardamom seeds on top. Cover the bowl and leave for about 12 hours so that the meat can absorb the flavour.

When ready for cooking, line a flat baking-dish with foil, place the breasts on top of the foil, pour over the marinade and seal the chicken tightly in the foil so that none of the juices can escape. Bake in a moderate oven, Gas Mark 4, 350°F, 180°C, for 25-30 minutes. Serve with a fennel and lemon salad (page 134).

Drunken chicken

The Chinese have a marvellous way of cooking chicken. They call it Drunken Chicken and that is exactly what it is – steeped in alcohol and left for days to soak it all up.

2¼ kg (5 lb) boiling chicken
2 spring onions
2-inch piece root ginger
1 bay leaf

250 ml (½ pint) Chinese rice wine
   or dry sherry
1¼ litres (2½ pints) water
5 teaspoons rock salt

Put the chicken in a large casserole breast side up and cover with the water until it is completely submerged. Peel and chop the ginger and slice all the spring onions including their green tops. Add the bay leaf, ginger and spring onions to the casserole and bring to the boil. Cover and simmer for about 20 minutes. Turn off the heat and leave the chicken in the casserole to cool in the water. Remove from the liquid when it is quite cold, skin and carve the chicken into small portions, rub it with the salt and arrange in a large flat dish. Strain the stock and reserve 250 ml (½ pint). (The rest can be used for other recipes). Mix the sherry with the stock and pour over the chicken. Cover the dish and leave in a cool place to soak up the juices for a minimum of 2-3 days before eating.

Duck

Ducks are by nature greedy birds. When killed in their prime between November and March, they have a layer of fatty tissue surrounding the meat. An excellent method for cooking duck is to steam roast it. This method allows all the fat to drain away while keeping the meat moist and the skin crisp.

Steam roasted duck stuffed with oranges

It is the bitter-sweet flavour of Seville oranges which acts as the perfect foil to roast duck. Sadly they have a limited season – from February to about mid-March – so as a substitute I suggest adding a dash of lemon juice or a teaspoon of vinegar to a sweet orange.

1 large duck
1 large onion, finely sliced
4 large Seville oranges
2 teaspoons 5-spice powder

pinch of cinnamon
salt and pepper to taste
125 ml (¼ pint) duck stock, made
   from giblets

Prepare the duck by wiping it dry, pulling away the loose fat and rubbing it liberally with a teaspoon of 5-spice powder mixed with a little salt. Prepare the stock from the giblets, setting aside the liver, according to the recipe for chicken stock on page 25. Strain and set aside. Slice the liver and season with salt and pepper. Grate the peel from the oranges, remove the pith and chop the fruit into small pieces. Heat the stock and cook the onions until transparent. Stir in 1 teaspoon of 5-spice powder, the cinnamon, liver, oranges and grated peel. Add enough stock to keep the mixture moist and simmer gently for about 3-4 minutes, taking care the oranges do not break up. Spoon the cooked stuffing into the duck and tie it up firmly. Place on a rack suspended over a dish of water and cook in a pre-heated oven, Gas Mark 9, 475°F, 240°C, for about 20 minutes. The skin should then be very crisp, so prick the bird all over with a fork to allow the fat to escape. Return to the oven and steam roast for a further 45 minutes or until cooked on Gas Mark 6, 400°F, 200°C. Serve hot using the stock as gravy.

Pickled duck

The Scandinavians have an unusual way of preparing duck which gives it a unique taste. The boned and skinned duck forms the centre-piece of the *smörgåsbord* – a tempting array of cold dishes for which Scandinavia is justly famous – and it is best eaten with a crisp salad.

1 plump duck	8 peppercorns
1 medium onion, stuck with cloves	130 g (5 oz) salt, mixed with
1 carrot, finely sliced	6 g (¼ oz) saltpetre (see note
5 bay leaves	overleaf)
8 juniper berries	4 tablespoons clear honey
1½ litres (3 pints) water	250 ml (½ pint) wine vinegar

If possible use a fresh bird, otherwise do make sure that it is well and truly defrosted and wiped dry before adding the marinade. Wipe dry both inside and outside, slash the skin with a sharp knife and rub the duck all over with salt and saltpetre mixed. Place in a casserole and cover with the carrot and onion. Meanwhile gently heat the honey with a little water until it is dissolved. Add the bay leaves, juniper berries and peppercorns and the rest of the water to make it up to 1½ litres (3 pints), and simmer covered for 5 minutes. Pour the liquid over the duck and leave to marinade for 3 days in a cool place, basting occasionally when you have a moment. The skin and outer layer of fat should be removed at the last moment before cooking, otherwise the flesh might harden, so loosen with a sharp knife and remove. Return the duck to the casserole and bake in a medium oven, Gas Mark 5, 375°F, 190°C, for about an hour or until tender. Carve the duck into small pieces and arrange on a dish. Strain the liquor and reduce by boiling vigorously until you have 500 ml (1 pint). Adjust the seasoning and pour over the duck. It can be eaten hot but it is traditionally left to cool before being served.

Note Most butchers are reluctant to sell saltpetre as it is distributed under licence. However, a good dispensing chemist should supply you, provided you are a known customer or that you can assure them that it is needed for pickling.

Game

By way of an afterthought I have added these three delicious recipes for pheasant, pigeon and rabbit. Rabbit is often ignored but it is a good, if slightly bony, buy. Pigeons are bred domestically and I am sure that if the demand increased they would be stocked by more obliging butchers and fishmongers. As for pheasant, sadly their season is limited and their cost is high, but the recipe is easily adapted for chicken.

Pheasant with curried apples

Pheasant is such a rare treat that it seems an indulgence to include a special recipe for it. However, the recipe works well with chicken, veal and rabbit or any meat which has a tendency to dryness.

1 large pheasant
6 Cox's apples, peeled, cored and sliced
1 teaspoon cinnamon
½ teaspoon curry powder

100 g (4 oz) *fromage blanc* (p.20)
1 glass Calvados (brandy or cider can be used)
125 ml (¼ pint) stock
salt and pepper to taste

Clean and prepare the pheasant, making sure that it is well hung (a rough guide is to allow 7-10 days depending on the warmth of the weather). In a heavy-based, enamelled casserole heat a little stock with the curry powder and brown the bird on all sides. Remove and set aside. In the same casserole arrange the apple slices in layers, sprinkle with the cinammon and put in the pheasant, with the breast facing downwards. Pour over the Calvados, cover with the remaining apple slices and bake covered in the oven, Gas Mark 4, 350°F, 180°C, for an hour. Turn the bird after half an hour and spoon over the sauce, making sure it is well covered. When it is cooked, remove the pheasant and place on a warm dish. Skim the gravy and pureé in a liquidizer, or pass through a sieve, with the *fromage blanc*, to form a rich sauce. Adjust the seasoning and serve with the pheasant.

Pigeon and red cabbage casserole

Wood pigeons – the plump gamey birds – are becoming increasingly difficult and expensive to buy. Luckily I have a friend who brings them up from Norfolk regularly during the season. The only trouble is that I then have to pluck, clean and dress them! An easier alternative is to buy the prepared pigeons, or squabs as they are sometimes called, which are on sale at most good butchers or poulterers.

4 pigeons	1 onion, finely chopped
1 onion, finely chopped	1 clove garlic
2 carrots, diced	juice and grated rind 2 oranges
1 celery stalk, diced	1 teaspoon honey
1 glass dry white wine	3 tablespoons wine vinegar
125 ml (¼ pint) stock	125 ml (¼ pint) stock
salt and pepper to taste	salt and pepper to taste
1 red cabbage – about 450 g (1 lb)	

Wipe the cleaned, dressed birds. In a heavy-based, enamelled casserole, heat the stock and add the chopped vegetables. Cook for a few minutes or until soft. Add the pigeons and turn them so that they are brown on all sides. Add the white wine, adjust the seasoning and bake in a warm oven, Gas Mark 3, 325°F, 170°C, for about 1½ hours.

To prepare the cabbage, wash and cut into fine slices and crush the clove of garlic with a little salt. In a separate pan heat the stock and add the onion, garlic and grated orange rind. Sweat for a few minutes and stir in the red cabbage. Pour over the orange juice, and the vinegar and add the salt, pepper and honey and simmer for about 2 hours, stirring occasionally. Stir the red cabbage in with the pigeons and return to the oven and bake for a further half-hour.

Note For a fuller flavour, cook the red cabbage a day in advance and leave to cool in its own juices before reheating.

Rabbit and mushrooms

Last summer while in Suffolk, I was taken on a rabbit expedition. The local gamekeeper decided to show the 'townies' just how easy it all was. To my utter amazement he drove off over the fields and proceeded to shoot the unsuspecting creatures without even emerging from his car – such was the sureness of his aim. The result was a rabbit stew of incredible freshness and flavour. If, however, you are forced to buy a rabbit, do marinade it for at least 2-3 hours, as it will make a great deal of difference.

1 rabbit	pinch of nutmeg
2 onions, chopped	1 teaspoon strong English mustard
1 clove garlic, crushed	2 glasses red wine
225 g (8 oz) mushrooms	125 ml (¼ pint) stock
1 teaspoon thyme	salt and pepper to taste

Joint the rabbit and spread thinly with the mustard. Pour over the red wine and sprinkle with garlic, thyme, nutmeg, salt and freshly ground black pepper. Leave to marinade, basting it occasionally for a minimum of 2 hours. When it is ready, heat a little stock in a heavy based, enamelled casserole. Cook the onions and when soft add the rabbit joints and turn them so that they brown on all sides to seal the flavour. Pour over the marinade, cover and simmer for about half an hour adding more stock if required. Add the mushrooms after half an hour, adjust the seasoning and leave all the ingredients to simmer gently until cooked. The liquid can either be puréed to form a thick sauce or left as it is and served poured over the meat.

Beef

Dr Johnson's morality was 'as English an article as a beef-steak' (Nathaniel Hawthorne). Beef is English, straightforward and part of our culinary culture. Huge sirloins, and juicy porter-houses, crisply roasted with no-nonsense trimmings, were forever served up and preferably by buxom wenches. Times and tastes have changed – the days of plain roast beef are on the decline as most of us can no longer afford to buy huge joints. But we have learnt to be more inventive as cooks, to copy other countries and buy cheaper cuts and create sauces to enhance the meat.

Hungarian goulash

The Hungarians are famous for their rhapsody and their goulash. The meat, a lean stewing steak such as chuck or shin, is slowly cooked in a piquant sauce and it deserves to rank among one of the great dishes of the world.

675 g (1½ lb) lean beef
1 large onion, chopped
1 tablespoon tomato purée
1 teaspoon caraway seeds
1 dessertspoon paprika
1 small carton stabilized yoghourt (p.19)
375 ml (¾ pint) stock
salt and pepper to taste
freshly chopped parsley

Cut the meat into 1-inch cubes and trim away the fat. Mix half the tomato purée with a little stock and heat in a heavy-based pan. Add the chopped onion and paprika, stirring continuously and pouring in more stock if required. Add the meat and brown on both sides, stir in the remainder of the tomato purée, the caraway seeds and enough stock to cover the meat. Add the salt and pepper as required. Cover and simmer or stew in a warm oven, Gas Mark 3, 325°F, 170°C, for about 2 hours. When cooked stir in the yoghourt and garnish with the freshly chopped parsley which provides a good strong colour contrast.

Manzo garafalato

This dish originates from Rome, where sadly there has never been a tradition of good beef. Most of it, it was rumoured, came from underfed, overworked oxen! The literal translation is cloved beef – the beef is studded with cloves and gently stewed in a rich tomato and wine sauce. As this dish was obviously invented to disguise the local disadvantages, any cheap lean cut can be used, but it should be left whole.

1¼-2 kg (3-4 lb) piece of beef (chuck steak or shin)
2 medium onions
2 cloves garlic
1 tablespoon tomato purée

6 to 8 cloves
1 teaspoon mixed spices
1 glass red wine
375 ml (¾ pint) beef stock
salt and pepper

Pierce the meat with a sharp knife or larding needle and insert the cloves at regular intervals. Sprinkle the meat with freshly ground black pepper and if necessary roll and tie it to make a tidy joint. In a heavy-based, iron casserole cook the onions and the garlic in a little of the stock. When brown add the meat and seal on both sides. Pour in the wine and heat until it has reduced by half. Combine the tomato purée with the mixed spice and stir it in with the meat. Cook for 3 minutes and then add just enough stock to cover the meat. Cover and gently simmer for 2½-3½ hours, adding more stock if the meat becomes too dry, by which time the meat will be incredibly tender and the sauce will have reduced to a dark, thick consistency.

Guinness stew

The Irish have a particularly interesting stew which is flavoured by Guinness. It is the equivalent of the French *daube,* where the meat is stewed for hours with herbs, vegetables and wine. The secret of a good casserole is to cook it well in advance and then gently to re-heat it so that the meat can thoroughly absorb the subtlety of the gravy.

1 kg (2 lb) stewing steak
1 large onion
225 g (8 oz) carrots
3 sticks celery
2 bay leaves
4 peppercorns

1 bouquet garni
1 teaspoon tomato purée
250 ml (½ pint) Guinness
125 ml (¼ pint) meat stock
salt and pepper to taste

Trim the meat and cut into cubes. Mix the tomato purée with a little stock, heat fiercely and brown the meat on all sides. Chop the vegetables into small cubes and put them into a good ovenproof casserole. Add the meat with the juice in which it has been browned, and the bay leaves, peppercorns and bouquet garni. Pour in the Guinness and sufficient stock to cover the meat. Adjust the seasoning, cover and cook for 2 hours at Gas Mark 3, 325°F, 170°C. Line the lid with a sheet of greaseproof paper to prevent evaporation, as unless the lid is a tight fit the stew may dry up. Stir it about every half-hour, adding more stock as necessary.

Beef in buttermilk

The Austrians have a particular method of dealing with poor-quality beef. They marinade it in buttermilk sharpened with capers and lemon rind and then bake it slowly in a clay pot or meat brick.

1¼-2 kg (3-4 lb) beef (any cheap cut)
2 medium onions, finely chopped
1 clove garlic

1 teaspoon capers
grated rind of 1 lemon
1 carton cultured buttermilk
salt and pepper to taste

Prepare the meat brick by soaking it in water for 15 minutes. Mix the buttermilk with the onions, capers, garlic and lemon rind and pour over the beef. Leave the meat to soak up the flavour for a minimum of 4 hours, turning it occasionally in the marinade.

Put the beef with the marinade into the prepared brick. Cover and bake at Gas Mark 6, 400°F, 200°C, for 2 hours. Remove the lid to allow the meat to brown and cook for a further 20 minutes. When cooked, carve the meat into thin slices and arrange on a dish. Strain the onions and liquidize with the capers to form a purée. Skim the gravy to remove the fat and reduce to half quantity. Stir into the purée and pour over the sliced meat.

Spiced beefburgers

I first tried a version of this dish in Morocco – it was prepared by our old cook Hanina, a shrieking tyrant who really knew how to cook. She would sally forth, heavily veiled, to the local market each week and it was from her that I learned how to pick the best vegetables. No 'don't touch' from the stall keepers – she would grab and squeeze with her fat strong hands until satisfied and then argue fiercely until a reasonable price was reached. She never trusted the butchers to prepare the meat, she insisted on mincing and pounding it herself with those amazing hands until the texture was just right – as smooth as dough. I learnt an awful lot from Hanina!

1 kg (2 lb) minced beef	1 tablespoon finely chopped
2 medium onions, finely grated	chervil
¼ teaspoon ground cumin	1 egg
¼ teaspoon ground coriander	salt and pepper to taste
¼ teaspoon ground cinnamon	

Mince the beef finely, putting it through the mincer at least twice. Mix the meat with all the other ingredients, kneading the meat thoroughly until it forms an almost paste-like consistency. Take a small amount of meat between the palms of your hands and press into the shape of flat balls. Pre-heat the grill and brush the metal tray with a little oil so that the meat will not stick. Grill the beefburgers for about 4 to 5 minutes on each side, depending on their thickness. They can also be cooked on a charcoal stove and are ideal for a summer barbecue.

Chinese meatballs

The Chinese cook their meatballs in sweet and sour sauce. This way the meat and the sauce acquire each other's flavour and the dish is a satisfying harmonious blend of tastes.

450 g (1 lb) minced beef
1 small onion, finely chopped
1 small green pepper
clove of garlic
pinch of ground ginger
pinch of 5-spice powder
1 egg

Gravy sauce:
500 ml (1 pint) beef stock or 500
    ml (1 pint) water with beef cube
    dissolved in it
1 tablespoon dry sherry
1 tablespoon soya sauce
salt and pepper to taste

Crush the clove of garlic with a little salt to form a fine paste. Set aside half of the garlic with the chopped onion and green pepper for the sauce. In a bowl mix the minced beef with the ginger and 5-spice powder and the onions and pepper. Beat the egg and add gradually to the mixture, stirring with a fork. The mince should be moist, but not too wet, so that it can be handled easily without sticking. Lightly dust your hands with flour, roll the meat between the palms of your hands to form little meatballs and place them on a sheet of greaseproof paper when ready for cooking.

Prepare the gravy by sweating the garlic, onions and pepper and a pinch of ground ginger in 3 tablespoons stock, stirring constantly to prevent them from burning. When soft add the remainder of the stock with the sherry and soya sauce. Heat until almost boiling and cook the meatballs for about 10 minutes in the liquid. Remove from the pan with a slotted spoon and reduce the sauce until it halves in quantity. Pour the sauce over the meatballs and serve immediately.

Beef curry

The Hindus have always had an ambivalent attitude to meat eating. 'To ask him if he eats meat, even when it is a well known fact that he does so, is to insult him deeply', wrote Abbé Dubois in the beginning of the nineteenth century, but when it came to the matter of beef they were far more direct: 'To kill a cow is not only a crime, but an awful sacrilege, a deicide, which can only be expiated by the death of the offender: while to eat of the flesh is a defilement which cannot be purified.' Not surprisingly, there are very few recipes for beef curry and most of these originate from North-Western India (now Pakistan) where a large proportion of the population is Muslim and therefore unhampered by such taboos.

675 g (1½ lb) frying steak, sliced and trimmed	½ teaspoon ground cinnamon
	2 cardamom seeds
2 medium onions, sliced	juice of ¼ lemon
2 cloves garlic	1 carton stabilized yoghourt
2 slices fresh ginger	2-3 tablespoons stock
1 dessertspoon ground coriander	salt and pepper to taste
½ teaspoon cumin powder	freshly chopped parsley

Chop the ginger and garlic and mash together with a little salt to make a thick paste. Add the coriander and the cumin, stir in the yoghourt and pour over the meat. Meanwhile heat the stock in a heavy-based, enamelled pan and sweat the onions. Add the cardamom and cinnamon and cook for a further minute so that the flavour of the spices is released. Add the meat with the spiced yoghourt, stirring gently. Cover and leave to cook on a low heat until the meat is tender. If the gravy is too thin and watery, remove the saucepan lid and allow the excess liquid to evaporate. Before serving add a dash of lemon juice and sprinkle with freshly chopped parsley.

Beef and walnut rolls

I was told by a discerning, if somewhat impoverished, gourmet that walnuts are an admirable substitute for truffles. This knowledgeable gentleman lived near a sprawling, prolific walnut tree and he was to be found at different times of the year gathering the crop. The green fruits were pickled according to a recipe which I have included on page 139. The slightly under-ripe nuts he would eat *en cerneau* – prepared with a dressing of salt, pepper, vinegar and shallots, whereas the ripe nuts were stored in brown paper to stop them drying up and either used in pounded puddings or eaten whole with a slice of cheese. The pickled walnuts, which incidentally can be bought from most shops, add a slightly woody flavour to the stuffing, which is suitable for either a whole and expensive fillet or, as in this recipe, individual stuffed and rolled slices.

1 kg (2 lb) lean beef (topside or rump)
1 dessertspoon Moutarde de Meaux
  (or any herbal mustard)

Stuffing
160 g (6 oz) minced veal
3 bacon rashers
1 medium onion

100 g (4 oz) mushrooms
6-8 pickled walnuts
1 teaspoon mixed herbs
1 egg
500 ml (1 pint) stock
½ glass red wine
salt and pepper to taste

Cut the beef into thin slices, beat with a wooden mallet until tender and spread each slice with a coating of mustard. To prepare the stuffing, roughly chop the mushrooms and onions. Trim the bacon rashers, discarding the rind and fat and cut into small pieces. Crush the pickled walnuts and mix all the ingredients with the veal. Add the herbs and salt and pepper as required. Beat the egg and stir into the mixture to bind the stuffing. Spread a little of this mixture on to each slice, and roll the meat loosely so that the stuffing is not pressed out at the sides. Secure the rolls with string or with a wooden toothpick and lay in an ovenproof dish. Pour over the stock and wine and cover. Bake in a warm oven, Gas Mark 3, 325°F, 170°C, for about 1 hour.

Grilled steak with green peppercorn sauce

Green peppercorns are so called because they are green in all senses of the word. Usually the berries, which grow in long clusters, are picked as soon as they turn red, laid out and left to wrinkle and blacken in the sun. Green peppercorns are picked before they are ripe and are immediately sealed in their own juices. They are soft to touch with a subtle flavour which lends a certain edge to this sauce. They can be bought from most delicatessen, but should you have any difficulty write to Provencal Food Merchants, 24 West Park Road, Kew, Richmond, Surrey, who import them direct from Madagascar.

4 rump steaks
1 teaspoon green peppercorns
100 g (4 oz) *fromage blanc* (p.20)

1 tablespoon white wine
salt to taste

Prepare the steaks by trimming away all the fat and, if the meat is not very tender, beating it with a wooden steak hammer. Mash the peppercorns with the wine to a thick paste. Pour half of the mixture over the steaks and leave to marinade for about 1 hour. Pre-heat the grill and cook the steak, allowing about 5-6 minutes for a rare steak. Pound the *fromage blanc* with the remainder of the peppercorns and stir in a tablespoon of the meat juices taken from the grill pan. Heat the sauce in a double saucepan, stirring continuously so that it does not separate. Pour the heated sauce over the steak and serve immediately.

Spiced beef

Spiced beef was a traditional Christmas dish long before the turkey was introduced to these shores. Its preparation is rather lengthy; Eliza Acton in her book *Modern Cookery for Private Families*, written in 1845, recommended curing the beef for 15 days until it was adequately seasoned for cooking. The following version is a good short cut. Laden with spices the brisket is almost pickled in a mixture of vinegar and water and then left to cool in the pungent liquid.

1¾-2 kg (3-4 lb) salt beef brisket	pinch of allspice
2 medium onions, chopped	4-6 peppercorns
2 large carrots, chopped	2 bay leaves
1 clove garlic	sprig of thyme
1 teaspoon powdered cloves	125 ml (¼ pint) vinegar
1 teaspoon ground ginger	500 ml (1 pint) water
pinch of nutmeg	

Combine all the spices and rub the mixture into the brisket. Leave it to stand for a minimum of 6 hours. When it is ready put it in a heavy saucepan, just large enough to contain all the ingredients, and cover with the vegetables. Put in the bay leaves, thyme, garlic and peppercorns and pour over the vinegar and water. Cover tightly and simmer gently for 3-4 hours or until the meat is thoroughly tender. If too much liquid evaporates in the cooking and the meat is in danger of burning add a mixture of 1 part vinegar and 3 parts water to the saucepan. Allow the meat to cool and then skim off the fat. The dish can either be re-heated or eaten cold with a crisp green salad.

Veal

Veal is a delicate tender meat which comes from a milk-fed calf slaughtered at an early age, between two and three months. There is still a certain reluctance on the part of many people to eat veal, left over from the days when they were slaughtered in the most appalling circumstances. In the interest of obtaining white flesh, the veal calf was bled day by day, until it was unable to stand and then, finally, killed.

Now more humane methods are used. The calf is slaughtered in much the same way as any animal, quickly with the minimum of pain. Young veal has little or no fat and needs careful cooking, otherwise the juices will dry out and the meat will be tough and flavourless. Whole joints are best steam-roasted or baked in a brick to ensure that all their moistness and flavour is retained.

Leg of veal

As there is little fat in a well-trimmed leg of veal, the juices are best preserved by either wrapping the joint in foil or cooking it in a meat brick.

1-1½ kg (2½-3½ lb) leg veal	1 glass dry white wine
1 teaspoon turmeric	juice of 1 orange
1 teaspoon ground rosemary	salt and pepper to taste
grated rind of 1 orange	

Prepare the meat brick, if required, by soaking it in water for 15 minutes. Mix the turmeric, rosemary, orange rind, and some freshly ground black pepper together and rub into the leg of veal. Pour over a glass of white wine and allow the joint to stand in the marinade for a minimum of 4 hours, but remember to baste it occasionally. Either place in a prepared meat brick, pouring over the marinade and bake in a slow oven, Gas Mark 2, 300°F, 150°C, or wrap the meat in foil to form a tight parcel and place on a baking-tray suspended over a dish filled with warm water. Cook in a slow oven, Gas Mark 2, 300°F, 150°C, for about 2½ hours. When cooked carefully undo the foil so that none of the juices escape. Skim the sauce into a saucepan, heat vigorously and add the orange juice, adjust the seasoning, remove from the heat and serve with the meat.

Braised veal

The idea of puréeing vegetables to make a sauce is not new. I have taken this recipe from Cassell's *Dictionary of Cooking* published in 1893, where they recommend this delicious method of cooking veal. Incidentally, the probable cost of veal then was 11d per pound.

1¼ kg (3 lb) veal (loin or best end of neck)
3 slices ham
1 carrot, sliced
1 teaspoon chopped mushrooms
1 onion, stuck with 2 cloves
1 clove garlic

small blade of mace
pinch of nutmeg
6 peppercorns
1 glass dry white wine
250 ml (½ pint) veal or chicken stock

Prepare the veal by chopping the bones short with a meat cleaver, or ask your butcher to do it for you, and remove the skin and any fat. Rub the base of a heavy saucepan or casserole with the cut clove of garlic. Lay two slices of ham on the bottom and place the veal on it. Add the carrot, onion, mushrooms, mace, nutmeg and peppercorns and cover the veal with the remaining slice of ham. Pour over the stock and cover the pan with a tight-fitting lid. Either simmer gently or bake in a warm oven, Gas Mark 3, 325°F, 170°C, until cooked, about 1½-2 hours. Remove the veal, carve into slices and arrange on a plate and keep warm in the oven. Skim the gravy and either liquidize or pass it through a sieve. Heat the purée with a glass of white wine. Pour over the veal and serve immediately.

Veal escalope with mushroom sauce

Jean Reynaud, the celebrated chef at Leith's restaurant, taught me this method of making a mushroom sauce. He was adamant about only puréeing raw mushrooms, otherwise the texture is too rubbery. The colour of the sauce is a pale pinky-grey which many people find unattractive. If this is the case use a drop of artificial colouring to brighten it up.

4 veal escalopes

100 g (4 oz) mushrooms

1 teaspoon oregano

160 g (6 oz) *fromage blanc* (p.00)

1 tablespoon veal or chicken stock

juice of ½ lemon

salt and freshly ground black pepper

Trim the escalopes and sprinkle with oregano and freshly ground pepper. Place under a pre-heated grill and cook on both sides, moistening occasionally with the lemon juice. Put the mushrooms, a pinch of oregano and the white cheese into a liquidizer. Add the stock, which should be cold, and whirr the ingredients together to form a smooth sauce. Gently heat the sauce in a double saucepan and pour over the veal. Serve immediately.

Veal with tuna fish sauce

This dish originates from Italy. It is a subtle blend of tuna fish, veal, capers, and lemon juice and makes an ideal summer meal, served with an endive salad. The Italians use fresh tuna caught from the Mediterranean but a tin will do just as well.

1-1½ kg (2½-3½ lb) boned leg of veal

2 anchovy fillets, cut into small pieces

1 onion, quartered

1 carrot, sliced

1 stick of celery, sliced

2 cloves garlic, cut into fine slivers

2-3 sprigs of parsley

6 peppercorns

water

lemon wedges

Sauce

1 small tin, 99 g (3½ oz), tuna fish

1 teaspoon drained capers

2 egg yolks

juice of 1 lemon

1 glass dry white wine

Prepare the meat by removing the skin and trimming away the excess fat. With a sharp knife make deep cuts all over the veal and insert a small piece of anchovy and a sliver of garlic into each incision. Roll and tie the meat securely and put in a saucepan with the vegetables, peppercorns, parsley and enough water to cover. There is no need to add extra salt as the anchovies will season the meat. Cover the pan and simmer for about 1½ hours.

When cooked, remove the veal and leave to cool. Carve into small slices and arrange on a dish.

To prepare the sauce add a glass of white wine to the stock, bring to the boil and reduce to make half a pint of liquid. Strain and set aside. Beat the egg yolks with the lemon juice. Gently heat this mixture in a double boiler, stirring constantly, adding the veal stock as the sauce thickens, to the consistency and colour of a mayonnaise. Drain the oil from the tuna fish and sieve or pound it until smooth. Stir into the sauce with the capers and extra lemon juice or white wine if required. The sauce should be fairly liquid. Adjust the seasoning and pour over the carved meat. Leave to cool and serve garnished with lemon wedges.

Veal and aubergine stew

Middle Eastern stews are usually richly flavoured with spices and fruit and are baked in slow ovens in half-glazed terracotta pots. Even nowadays many houses do not have their own ovens and so the women take their dishes to the local baker who cooks them in his large clay-lined oven after he has made the bread for the day.

675 g (1½ lb) stewing veal, cut into 1-inch cubes
2 medium sized aubergines
1 large onion, finely chopped
3-4 tomatoes, skinned and roughly chopped, or 1 small tin, 226 g (8 oz), tomatoes
1 tablespoon tomato purée
½ teaspoon ground cumin
½ teaspoon allspice
125 ml (¼ pint) veal or chicken stock
1 tablespoon water
salt and pepper

Cut the aubergines into thick slices and sprinkle with salt. Leave to stand in a colander with a weight on top so that the bitter juices can drain away. After half an hour wash the aubergines and pat dry with a kitchen cloth.

Mix a little of the tomato purée with the water and heat. Cook the onions in this mixture, stirring constantly and adding more water as required. Add the veal and brown with the onions. Pour in the stock with the remaining ingredients and carefully lay the aubergines on the top. Adjust the seasoning, cover and place in a slow oven, Gas Mark 2, 300°F, 150°C, and cook for about 1½ hours until the meat is tender.

Stuffed shoulder of veal

1 shoulder of veal weighing 1¼-2 kg (3-4 lb)
1 small tin, 200 g (7 oz), artichoke hearts
225 g (8 oz) tomatoes, peeled and roughly chopped
2 onions, finely chopped
large pinch of lemon balm
grated rind and juice of 1 lemon
1 bay leaf
6 peppercorns
250 ml (½ pint) chicken stock (see note below)

Prepare the meat brick, if required, by soaking in water for 15 minutes. Bone the shoulder of veal, trim the excess fat and lay it flat. Strain the artichokes and roughly chop. In a bowl mix the artichokes with the peeled and chopped tomatoes, onions, lemon balm and grated lemon rind. Add salt to taste and a touch of freshly ground black pepper. Spoon about three-quarters of the stuffing on to the veal, roll it and tie securely. Do not worry if any of the stuffing falls out, spread it with a knife over the rolled sides. Put the remainder of the mixture into a casserole, place the veal on top and pour over the lemon juice and stock. Add the bay leaf, peppercorns and another pinch of lemon balm. Cover tightly and cook at Gas Mark 3, 325°F, 170°C, for 1½-2 hours. When cooked remove the veal, skim the gravy and serve either puréed with the vegetables or as a thin sauce.

Note If this recipe is cooked in a meat brick you do not need to add any stock as the veal will cook in its own juices.

Spiced veal loaf

I have included two recipes for baked veal loaf – in the first the veal is mixed with spinach and a selection of herbs and is like a pâté eaten as an hors-d'oeuvre (see page 49). Spiced veal is much richer and is probably more suitable as a main course, although there is nothing to stop you trying them the other way around.

1 kg (2 lb) minced veal
2 medium onions, grated
2 cloves garlic, mashed with salt
small tin tomato purée
1 teaspoon ground mixed spices (allspice, cloves, mace)
pinch of cinnamon
125 ml (¼ pint) water

Mince the veal a minimum of twice and then pound in a pestle and mortar with the onion, garlic and mixed spices to form a paste. Grease the inside of the loaf tin and spoon in the mixture. Cover the tin with tin foil and stand in a baking-dish filled with water. Cook for about 45 minutes at Gas Mark 4, 350°F, 180°C. Mix the tomato purée, cinnamon and water, remove the foil from the meat and pour over the tomato juice. Cook uncovered until all the tomato juice has been absorbed, 10-15 minutes, and the loaf starts to form a crisp crust. Do not overcook as the meat will dry out. Turn out of the tin and serve cut into slices with a spicy tomato sauce if required.

Veal chops with cucumber

4 veal chops
½ cucumber, peeled and sliced
   lengthways into ½-inch slices
½ teaspoon dill
pinch of cayenne pepper

1 carton stabilized yoghourt (p.19)
250 ml (½ pint) veal or chicken
   stock
salt and pepper to taste

Trim the chops, removing all traces of fat. Heat a little stock in a pan and cook the chops until brown on both sides. Add the cucumber with the dill and the remainder of the stock. Adjust the seasoning, cover the pan and stew gently for about half an hour until the meat is cooked. Remove the meat and cucumber and keep warm. Reduce the stock by half and pour in the yoghourt. Heat gently and pour over the veal. Sprinkle with the cayenne pepper to add a touch of colour.

Lamb

In Victorian times large estates and country houses used to keep house lambs to ensure an almost constant supply of lamb. They were born in the middle of the winter, reared under shelter, fed mainly on milk and eaten from Christmas until Lady Day. At Easter the first of the grass lambs would come into season and they would last until September or October.

Nowadays, what with freezers and vast imports from New Zealand, lamb need no longer be a seasonal dish and can be eaten all year long. Mutton which is the meat from a sheep is almost impossible to buy in the shops, which may be just as well as it is, by all accounts, a rather fat-laden if tasty meat.

Do trim lamb thoroughly before cooking, discarding all the fat. The French are very particular about trimming their *gigot*, and I agree with them, for not only does it obviously reduce the fat content, but the meat from a trimmed lamb has a much cleaner and fresher taste.

Roast garlic lamb

The French have a reputation for using garlic, and plenty of it, with everything. Apart from adding an exquisite flavour, they maintain that it aids digestion, purifies the blood and keeps the eyes bright and shining.

1 leg of lamb weighing 1¼-2 kg (3-4 lb)
3-4 cloves garlic
sprig of rosemary

Wipe the leg of lamb with a dry cloth and trim away all the fat. Peel the cloves of garlic and cut into thin slivers. With the point of a sharp knife, spear a sliver and insert into the lamb. How much garlic you use will depend on your taste, but in my opinion you cannot overdo it: the lamb should be studded with garlic. Place the lamb on a wire rack suspended over a baking-tray filled with water. Sprinkle the rosemary over the joint and place in a pre-heated oven, Gas Mark 8, 450°F, 230°C, and sear for 15 minutes to seal the flavour. Turn the oven down to Gas Mark 5, 375°F, 190°C, and cook for a further hour. Carve and serve immediately.

Mustard-coated shoulder of lamb

. Moutarde de Meaux Pommery is my favourite of all French mustards. The story is that in 1760, a superior of the ancient religion of Meaux gave the recipe to the Pommery family and they have produced it ever since. It is a closely guarded secret blend of mustard seed and spices with a tantalizing flavour. Brillat-Savarin once called it the mustard for gourmets. It is now sold in this country in most good food shops; it is not cheap but then you do not need to use a lot, so a jar should last a long time.

1 shoulder lamb, 1¼-2 kg (3-4 lb) with bone
Coating:
2 medium onions
1 clove garlic, crushed

½ teaspoon rosemary
1 teaspoon mixed herbs
1 tablespoon Moutarde de Meaux (or good herbal mustard)
salt and pepper to taste

Bone the shoulder of lamb and trim away all the fat and lay the meat skin side down on a flat surface. Grate the onions finely and mix with the garlic, herbs, mustard and salt and pepper to taste. Spread about two-thirds of the coating over the inside of the lamb, and roll up the meat as you would a Swiss roll. Secure with skewers or tie at regular intervals with string. Now spread the remainder of the stuffing all over the outside of the meat. Place the lamb on a rack suspended over a baking-tray filled with water and put in a pre-heated oven, Gas Mark 5, 375°F, 190°C, and cook for about 1 hour or longer, depending on how rare you like your meat.

Note This coating can also be spread over lamb chops before they are grilled.

Marinaded lamb

Lamb marinaded in wine with a few vegetables and herbs acquires the tantalizing gamey taste of venison. This dish does admittedly require a little organization as the lamb should be marinaded a minimum of 4 days before cooking – but once you have initially prepared it all you have to do is occasionally turn it in its marinade to ensure that all sides of the meat soak up the flavours. So it really is not too much trouble.

1 leg of lamb weighing
 1½-2 kg (3-4 lb)
salt

Marinade:
3 carrots, sliced
2 onions, sliced
2 cloves garlic, sliced

1 teaspoon rosemary
½ teaspoon marjoram
3-4 parsley stalks
3-4 bay leaves
8-10 juniper berries
6-8 black peppercorns
125 ml (¼ pint) red wine vinegar
500 ml (1 pint) red wine

Trim away all the fat from the leg of lamb and wipe with a dry cloth. Lay the meat flat in a non-corrosive dish – stainless steel, porcelain or glass – which is just large enough to fit the joint. Cover the meat with the vegetables. Mix the remaining ingredients for the marinade together and pour it over the meat. Leave in a cool place and turn and baste it about 2 or 3 times a day in its dish. After a while the joint will turn a pink-purple colour as it soaks up the marinade. When it is ready to be cooked, remove from the dish and strain the vegetables and herbs. Line the bottom of an ovenproof baking-dish with the vegetables and lay the joint on top. Sprinkle with a little salt and place in a pre-heated oven, Gas Mark 8, 450°F, 230°C, to sear the meat. After 15 minutes reduce the heat to Gas Mark 5, 375°F, 190°C, and cook, basting occasionally with the marinade for a further hour or until tender. When cooked, remove the joint and keep warm. Skim off the fat and strain the vegetables. Liquidize in a blender or a vegetable mouli to form a purée. Add about 2-3 tablespoons of the skimmed gravy to the purée. Serve hot with the lamb.

Lamb chops with apricot sauce

King Henry VIII, in his constant search for new and exciting foods to stimulate his jaded appetite, was responsible for introducing the apricot to England. It was grown in the sheltered walled gardens at Hampton Court and then transported by barge up the River Thames to be served at his table.

4-6 loin or chump chops
salt and pepper to taste
pinch of ground cumin

Sauce:
225 g (8 oz) dried apricots
½ teaspoon cinnamon
¼ teaspoon ground cumin
slice of lemon peel
water

Trim the chops and remove all traces of fat. Sprinkle with cumin and freshly ground pepper and grill under a pre-heated grill until cooked. To prepare a sauce soak the apricots for a minimum of 4 hours in water, or cold weak tea if preferred, to add extra flavour, until soft. Drain and put in a saucepan with the cinnamon, cumin, lemon peel and enough water to cover. Cover and stew until tender. Pass the sauce through a sieve, or liquidize and serve poured over the lamb chops.

Steamed lamb with coriander

Coriander was first introduced to England by the Romans. It seems to have had a variety of uses ranging from curing spotty faces to flavouring certain alcoholic liquors. It is also known as 'dizzy corn' because it relieves dizziness when seeds are crushed and the aroma inhaled. Both the leaves and seeds are used for flavouring.

450 g (1 lb) lean lamb
1 onion, finely chopped
1 clove garlic, crushed
1 teaspoon coriander seeds, crushed

1 carton stabilized yoghourt (p.19)
salt and pepper to taste
freshly chopped coriander leaves

Use either a boned leg or shoulder of lamb for this recipe. Trim away the fat and cut the meat into 1-inch cubes. Arrange on a steamer with the onions and salt and pepper. If you do not have a steamer, balance a colander over a saucepan of water; but make sure that whatever container you use has sufficient holes to allow the lamb fat to drain away. Steam the meat gently for about 45 minutes until tender. Heat the yoghourt and stir in the garlic and crushed coriander seeds. Simmer for a few minutes to release the flavour of the spices and add the cooked lamb. Simmer for a further 5 or 10 minutes and serve immediately, garnished with chopped coriander leaves.

Lamb curry

I shall never forget walking through the spice bazaar early one morning before the sun was too hot in Jaipur. There was so much to see and smell: Rajput women in their colourful cholis or sari blouses grinding freshly dried scarlet chillies on their chakkis or grinding stones, my eyes and nose streaming from the pungent aroma as I watched; piles of turmeric, a bold yellow against the dark richness of cloves, cinnamon sticks emitting a soothing scent and the golden brown of nutmeg contrasting with the mounds of white and black peppercorns.

675 g (1½ lb) lean lamb	½ teaspoon chilli powder
1 onion, sliced	½ teaspoon cinnamon
2 cloves garlic	½ teaspoon turmeric
1-inch piece fresh root ginger	1 large carton, 454 g (16 fl. oz)
2 cardamom pods	stabilized yoghourt (p.19)
2 cloves	125 ml (¼ pint) stock

Trim the lamb, remove all the fat and cut into cubes. Wash the meat in a sieve under a running cold tap and drain thoroughly before use. Peel the ginger and garlic and pound in a pestle and mortar with a little salt to form a smooth paste. This can also be done by putting them in a plastic bag and crushing them with a wooden rolling-pin. Crack the cardamom pods to release the little black seeds and add the seeds only with the chilli, cinnamon and turmeric to the paste. Stir the mixture into the yoghourt and simmer gently for a few minutes but do not boil. Meanwhile, heat a little stock in a heavy-based, enamelled pan and cook the onions until tender. Add the meat and cloves and brown on all sides. Pour the yoghourt over the meat, cover the pan and simmer on a very low heat for about 45 minutes. You may have to add a little stock to prevent the sauce from drying up. Remove the cloves and serve immediately.

Note This dish is very heavily spiced and you may find that it is too hot, in which case use the chilli powder and ginger very sparingly.

Red cooked lamb

Chinese cookery is based on complicated and intricate preparation and quick cooking, primarily because the Chinese always suffered from a shortage of fuel and so did their utmost to conserve their supplies. Red cooking is an exception, the meat is gently simmered in a rich soya sauce which as it thickens to form a rich gravy turns an astonishing colour.

675 g (1½ lb) lean lamb
1 onion, sliced
1-inch piece of fresh root ginger, peeled and grated
¼ teaspoon 5-spice powder
peel of half an orange, pared and sliced

2 tablespoons soya sauce
1 tablespoon dry sherry
250 ml (½ pint) stock
chopped spring onion

Trim the lamb and cut away all the fat, cut into thin slices. Rub the ginger and 5-spice powder into the meat. Heat a little of the stock in a heavy-based, enamelled saucepan and sweat the onion and orange peel. Add the prepared meat and the soya sauce and sherry and slowly bring to the boil, stirring continuously so that the meat does not burn or stick to the bottom. Stir in the remainder of the stock and allow it to come to the boil. Skim the liquid to get rid of any fat or scum, cover and gently simmer until the meat is so tender that it is starting to flake. Remove the meat from the pan and keep warm. Reduce the liquid by vigorously boiling until it forms a thick sauce. Remove the peel and pour the sauce over the meat. Serve garnished with freshly chopped spring onions.

Courgettes stuffed with lamb

10 or 12 medium courgettes

½ teaspoon allspice
pinch of nutmeg

Stuffing:
450 g (1 lb) lean minced lamb
1 onion, finely chopped
1 clove garlic, chopped

125 ml (¼ pint) tomato juice, *or* 1
teaspoon tomato purée made up
with water
salt and pepper to taste

Wash the courgettes and sprinkle with a little salt to soften them. Leave to drain in a colander for about half an hour and wash and dry thoroughly. With a sharp knife cut off the top of each courgette and carefully scoop out the pulp so as not to break the skin. Meanwhile, heat a little of the tomato juice in a heavy-based, enamelled saucepan and sweat the onion and garlic until tender. Stir in the minced lamb and allspice and simmer together for about 10 minutes. Remove from the heat and drain the meat into a sieve, pressing firmly against the sides with a wooden spoon to extract all the fat. Mash the pulp from the courgettes and mix with the meat. Adjust the seasoning and stuff the whole courgettes with the mixture. Lay the courgettes side by side in a flat-bottomed ovenproof dish. Pour over the remaining tomato juice, sprinkle with nutmeg, cover and bake in a moderate oven, Gas Mark 4, 350°F, 180°C, for about half an hour or until the vegetables are tender.

Aubergines stuffed with lamb

6 medium aubergines
stuffing as in previous recipe

To prepare the aubergines, wash thoroughly and cut into half lengthways. Scoop out the centres and sprinkle both the skins and pulp with salt. Leave to drain for about half an hour, wash and dry thoroughly. Continue as you would in the previous recipe, using the pulp from the aubergines to mix in with the stuffing.

Green peppers stuffed with lamb

6 green peppers
stuffing as in recipe for stuffed courgettes plus 100 g (4 oz) mushrooms

Wash the green peppers and dry thoroughly; with a sharp knife cut off their tops and scoop out the seeds. Blanch the peppers in boiling salted water for about 5 minutes, drain and refresh in cold water. Proceed exactly as you would in the recipe for stuffed courgettes, adding the chopped tops of the green peppers and the sliced mushrooms to the filling.

Lamb kebabs

Lamb is primarily used for kebabs because it is the meat most readily available in the Middle East and partly because its texture is the most suitable for grilling over a charcoal stove. There are various kinds of kebab sticks on sale. At a pinch ordinary meat skewers will do, but they tend to get too hot to handle. My favourites come from Morocco. The handles are crudely carved from cedar wood and are dipped into water before use. Not only does it keep them cool but as the wood dries out from the heat it emits the rich heady smell of cedar. They are imported into this country and I must declare my interest here, because I sell them in my kitchen shop in London, off Portobello Road.

1 kg (2 lb) lean lamb (shoulder or leg)	*Marinade:*
	1 onion
2 medium onions	1 clove garlic
4 firm tomatoes	large pinch of oregano
2 medium green peppers	juice of 1 lemon
	1 carton low-fat yoghourt
	salt and pepper to taste

Trim the lamb, remove all the fat and cut into 1-inch cubes. For the marinade, chop the onion and garlic and crush in a garlic or fruit press to extract their juices. In a large bowl mix the yoghourt, lemon juice and oregano, together with the onion and garlic juice and salt and pepper to taste. Add the meat and stir thoroughly so that it is well and truly coated with the marinade. Leave to marinade in a cool place for a minimum of 2 to 4 hours. When the meat is ready, cut the onions and tomatoes into quarters and blanch the green peppers in boiling water for a few minutes before cutting into slices. Thread the meat on to the kebab sticks, alternating it with slices of the onions, tomatoes or green pepper. Cook under a pre-heated grill or over an open glowing charcoal fire. Depending on how rare you like your meat it should take about 7 minutes. Turn the kebab sticks while cooking and baste occasionally with the marinade. Serve with fresh green salad.

Pork

Pork was at one time thought to be unsuitable to eat during the hot weather as it was considered particularly liable to disease. The ideal season was between November and March and the pigs were reared accordingly.

Nowadays, with modern refrigeration and cold store rooms, such precautions are quite unnecessary and it is quite safe to eat pork all the year around. There are a variety of good cuts to choose from: leg, shoulder, loin and spare rib are the leanest and best known. Pork does, however, have a tendency to be rather fatty, so make sure that it is carefully trimmed before cooking. It should be cooked thoroughly for, unlike red meat, it is not improved by being served slightly rare.

Roast leg of pork

Pork is the one meat which can be marinaded in a salt rub. Cassell's *Dictionary of Cookery* explains: 'All meats are not rendered equally salt or hard by exposure to the action of salt. Pork becomes less salt than beef.' Therefore, because it absorbs less salt, it will not shrink or harden during cooking. The quality of the salt used is important as 'different kinds of salt seem to differ in their degree of saltness, as one sugar is sweeter than another.' I use rock salt crystals which I crush together with peppercorns, herbs and spices in a pestle and mortar. This dry marinade tenderizes the meat and enhances the flavours.

leg of pork weighing 1½-2 kg (3½-4½ lb)
1½ teaspoons salt
6-8 black peppercorns
large pinch of ground thyme

large pinch of marjoram
large pinch of rosemary
2 bay leaves
½ teaspoon allspice

Prepare the leg of pork *à la mode française,* cut off the rind with a sharp knife, trim the fat to a thin layer and prick the joint all over with a fork. This sadly means no crackling, but the sharpness of the flavour of the meat will more than compensate. Grind the salt with the peppercorns, herbs and allspice until they are thoroughly mixed together and rub into the pork, covering all the surfaces. Leave for a minimum of 4 hours – but as with most marinaded meat, the longer the better – remove the excess salt with a dry cloth and place the joint on a grid over a baking-dish filled with water. Cook for 2½-2¾ hours in a moderate oven, Gas Mark 4, 350°F, 180°C.

Pork chops with apple and sage

Sage is sadly neglected nowadays, usually relegated to the role of sage and onion stuffing; traditionally it was served with goose, duck and pork as it was supposed to help the stomach digest the rich meat. It was also a much favoured herb and according to an old English proverb:

He that would live for Aye
Must eat Sage in May.

obviously when the leaves were at their most potent!

4-6 pork chops
2 medium onions, sliced
2 medium cooking apples, peeled, cored and sliced

4-5 sage leaves, *or* 1 teaspoon dried sage
1 tablespoon stock
1 glass white wine, *or* dry cider
salt and pepper to taste

Trim away the fat from the pork chops. Heat the stock in a

heavy-based, enamelled pan and cook the onions until soft. Add the pork chops, brown on both sides and remove. Arrange the apple slices and sage in layers with the onions and pork and pour the wine over them. Adjust the seasoning. Cover the pan and cook on a low heat, stirring occasionally for a further 20-25 minutes until the pork is cooked.

Remove the meat from the pan and keep warm. Skim off the excess fat and pass the vegetables through a sieve or liquidize to make a smooth sauce. Pour the sauce over the meat and serve.

Pork roll

Stuffed and rolled loin of pork is equally delicious served hot or left to cool in its own gravy to form a jelly, but the fat must be skimmed off before it sets. As in the preceding recipe sage is the predominant flavour though fresh basil can be substituted as an alternative. Ask your butcher to bone and skin a loin of pork but leave it unrolled.

1¼-2 kg (3-4 lb) boned loin of pork
450 g (1 lb) tomatoes, peeled and chopped
2 onions, finely sliced
2 cloves garlic
1 teaspoon ground sage

1 teaspoon salt
½ teaspoon freshly ground black pepper
2 tablespoons stabilized yoghourt (p.19)

Prepare the meat brick by soaking in water for 15 minutes. Mash the garlic with the salt, pepper and sage to the consistency of paste. Add about half of the tomatoes and mix together. Spread two-thirds of this mixture over the inside surface of the pork and roll it up as you would a Swiss roll and tie securely with string. Place the onions and the rest of the tomatoes in the prepared brick. Lay the meat on the bed of vegetables and spread the rest of the paste over it. Bake in a hot oven, Gas Mark 9, 475°F, 240°C, for about 1½ hours. Remove from oven and carve the meat into thin slices, skim off the excess fat and strain the vegetables and liquidize with about 2 tablespoons of the meat's juices or enough to make a purée. Stir in the yoghourt and pour over the meat or serve separately as gravy.

Steamed pork with juniper berries

The juniper berry is the fruit of a small prickly shrub and it takes two to three years to ripen to a bluish-black hue before it is ready to be eaten. The green berries are far too bitter to eat, but I remember seeing a branch nailed to a stable door in Northern Italy; it was protection against the Devil, used in the same way as we would a horseshoe. The ripe berries blend well with pork and I especially like the contrast of colours in this recipe.

450 g (1 lb) boned loin or boned leg pork	8-10 juniper berries
450 g (1 lb) sliced leeks	pinch of powdered thyme
1 small sliced onion	juice of half a lemon
	salt and pepper to taste

Trim the meat and cut into small cubes. Crush the juniper berries with the back of a wooden spoon and mix with the lemon juice and thyme. Pour the mixture over the meat and set aside. Cut the leeks and onion into rings and wash thoroughly. Arrange the vegetables on a heatproof plate and lay the meat on top with the berries. Adjust the seasoning. Cover and steam for about 25 minutes until the meat is tender.

Pork fillet with herbs

Adapted from Elizabeth David's book *Spices, Salt and Aromatics in the English Kitchen* (pp.181-2 © Elizabeth David, 1970). Miss David uses the mixture instead of a sugar glaze or breadcrumbs on a joint of middle gammon, or as a stuffing for fresh baked pork. It also works well as a filling for pork fillet, especially if you use as many fresh herbs as possible. But if you haven't got round to growing your own yet, make do with dried.

3-4 pork fillets	1 teaspoon crushed coriander seeds
1 glass white wine	1 teaspoon marjoram
juice of 1 lemon	½ teaspoon freshly ground black pepper
Stuffing:	
1 teaspoon mint	3 tablespoons breadcrumbs
1 teaspoon fresh parsley	grated peel of 1 lemon
1 teaspoon lemon thyme	grated peel of half an orange
1 teaspoon chives	1 egg

Prepare the fillets by splitting them about half-way through lengthways with a sharp knife, beat with the flat end of a meat hammer and set aside. Cut the fresh herbs into small pieces with a pair of scissors and mix with the pepper, coriander, grated peel and the remaining dried herbs. Beat the egg with the breadcrumbs and pour into the mixture, stirring to form the stuffing. Spread it between the pork fillets, making sure that it doesn't spill out. Secure each fillet with poultry pins or wooden toothpicks and place in a flat roasting-dish. Pour the wine and lemon juice over the pork and roast at Gas Mark 4, 350°F, 180°C, for about 1¼ hours, basting frequently. Remove the poultry pins and serve the meat carved into slices.

Pork chops with purée of pears

Pears in red wine is a great family favourite and I have adapted the taste to go with pork. The addition of fennel gives the dish a fresher quality reminiscent of raw *finocchio* eaten in Italian salad days. One word of advice, use unripe pears as the acid changes to sugar when baked, so ripe pears will make the dish too sweet.

4 pork chops
450 g (1 lb) unripe pears, peeled, cored and chopped
1 small bulb of fennel roughly chopped

1 glass red wine
1 tablespoon stock
salt and pepper to taste

Trim away the fat from the pork chops. Using a heavy-based, enamelled casserole sweat the fennel in the stock. Remove and brown the chops in the same pan, adding more stock if necessary. Cover the meat with the fennel and pears and pour over the glass of red wine. Adjust the seasoning. Bake in a moderate oven, Gas Mark 4, 350°F, 180°C, for about 50 minutes. Remove the meat. Pour off the fat and purée the vegetables in a liquidizer or pass through a sieve. Serve the purée as an accompanying sauce.

Chinese spare ribs

The first time I attempted to buy spare ribs, I was shown a rather bony joint. As I peered rather blankly at it, my butcher said knowingly, 'You must mean Chinese spare ribs, not the same thing at all. This piece comes from the shoulder and very succulent it is too.' Having been put right I pass on this conversation only to avoid any further confusion.

Chinese spare ribs or short ribs are rather greasy unless cooked properly. They should be roasted in a hot oven, suspended from the shelf by butchers' hooks inserted at each end so that the fat can drain off. The hooks can be bought from most kitchen or hardware shops but a piece of wire bent into an S-shape will do.

1 kg (2 lb) Chinese spare ribs in one piece	1 teaspoon Worcestershire sauce
Marinade:	1 teaspoon vinegar
3 tablespoons soya sauce	2 cloves garlic
1 tablespoon dry sherry	2 slices root ginger
1 tablespoon honey	½ teaspoon salt

Trim away any excess fat and place the ribs in a shallow dish. Crush the garlic with the salt and ginger with the flat edge of a knife to form a paste. Combine the remaining ingredients with the paste and cook over a low heat until the honey has melted. Pour over the meat and leave to marinate for 4 hours, basting and turning every half-hour. Pre-heat the oven to Gas Mark 8, 450°F, 230°C, and on the bottom shelf place a baking-dish half filled with water to catch the drips. When the spare ribs have thoroughly soaked up the marinade, pierce each end with a butcher's hook, and attach the hooks to the top shelf of the oven. Cook for about 40 minutes. The spare ribs should be crisp but not too dry, so they may need basting with the marinade. To serve, separate meat with a meat cleaver or sharp knife into individual portions.

Liver

Calves' liver is considered to be the finest and is by far the most expensive. Lambs' liver is cheaper and a more than adequate substitute: pigs' and ox liver are only suitable for pâtés and heavily spiced stews. Chicken livers can be bought frozen and are extremely tasty and exceptionally good value.

Mint liver

I grew up, like many people, refusing to eat liver. I had been forced to eat it as a child as I was constantly told that it was good for me – enough to put anybody off for life. It wasn't until I went to the Lebanon that I had to eat it again; it was served at a dinner party and I couldn't risk offending my host. I did, however, enjoy it so much that I even begged the recipe from the cook and here is my version.

675 g (1½ lb) lambs' liver, finely sliced
1 large onion, finely chopped
1 clove garlic, crushed

1 tablespoon finely chopped fresh mint
125 ml (¼ pint) wine vinegar
250 ml (½ pint) chicken stock

Brown the liver in a little stock and remove from the pan. Add the onions and garlic and more stock if required and cook until soft. Add the vinegar and mint and stir together. Replace the meat in the pan, adjust the seasoning and cover. Simmer for about 10 minutes until the liver is cooked.

Liver en papillote

Papillote means a little parcel. The liver is stuffed, wrapped in foil or greaseproof paper before cooking. This method is similar to baking in a clay pot or brick and is more practical for smaller cuts of meat.

675 g (1½ lb) lambs' liver, cut into slices
100 g (4 oz) mushrooms
1 medium onion, finely chopped
1 clove garlic, crushed

large pinch of thyme
6 peppercorns, crushed
juice of 1 lemon
2 tablespoons cultured buttermilk

Cut the liver into thin slices and put in a flat dish. Combine the buttermilk with half the lemon juice and half the quantity of peppercorns and thyme. Pour the mixture over the liver and marinade for 2-3 hours. To prepare the stuffing combine the mushrooms, garlic, onion and remainder of the peppercorns, thyme and lemon juice. Remove the liver from the marinade and lay each slice on a sheet of foil or greasproof paper. Dribble the stuffing over the meat and fold over the paper, making sure that you leave plenty of air in the parcel. Secure it and place in a baking-tray in the oven, Gas Mark 4, 350°F, 180°C. Bake for 20-30 minutes until cooked. Serve still wrapped so that none of the juice is lost.

Chicken liver with tarragon

There are two kinds of tarragon, French and Russian, and they are not to be confused. French is the true tarragon, sweet and tangy and ideal for cookery and can be bought fresh or dried, whereas the Russian variety is rather bitter and should not be used as a culinary herb. Practically all dried tarragon is of the French variety and as the herb jars are clearly marked there should be no difficulty in distinguishing what you are buying.

450 g (1 lb) chicken livers	grated rind of 1 orange
1 onion, sliced	juice of 1 orange
1 clove garlic	salt and pepper to taste
½ teaspoon tarragon	250 ml (½ pint) chicken stock

Trim the livers, pour over the orange juice and sprinkle with freshly ground pepper. Heat a little stock and sweat the onions and garlic. Stir in the grated orange rind and tarragon and cook for a further minute. Add the liver with the orange juice and brown. Pour in sufficient stock to cover the meat and simmer for about 5 minutes or until the liver is tender. It should be browned on the outside but the flesh should still be slightly pink. Serve immediately as liver toughens if re-heated.

Kidneys

Kidneys are classed as offal – a word which does no justice to their delicious taste. Veal kidneys are the most delicately flavoured and lamb are slightly stronger. Personally I find pig and ox kidneys far too strong, but I have read that if plunged in boiling water for a second they are rendered less pungent.

To prepare kidneys remove the outer casing of fat and peel off the outer membrane. Slice in two lengthways and remove the core. Some recipes advise cooking the kidneys whole but they absorb far less flavour that way. One thing to avoid is overcooking. They need only a few minutes, cooking over a gentle heat, otherwise they become far too tough and virtually inedible.

Kidneys in wine and tomato sauce

12 kidneys (allow 2-3 per person)
1 large onion, sliced
1 clove garlic
1 small tin, 226 g (8 oz) tomatoes
1 teaspoon tomato purée
large pinch of basil

1 glass red wine
2 tablespoons stabilized yoghourt
 (p.19)
125 ml ($\frac{1}{4}$ pint) chicken stock
salt and pepper to taste

Prepare the kidneys according to the directions above. Strain the tinned tomatoes and heat the juice in a frying-pan. Cook the onions and garlic until soft, adding the stock if necessary, and stir in the tomato purée. Add the basil, the strained tomatoes and the glass of red wine, and adjust the seasoning. Simmer gently until all the flavours have mixed together and then add the kidneys. Simmer for about 5-7 minutes and when cooked stir in 2 tablespoons of yoghourt. Serve immediately.

Grilled kidney kebabs

Grilled kidneys make interesting kebabs, especially when marinaded with mushrooms, onions and crushed fennel seeds. Use whole small pickling onions for kebabs, they look more attractive and are much easier to thread on to the sticks.

12 kidneys
225 g (8 oz) mushrooms
24 pickling onions (allow 4 per
  kebab)

Marinade:
1 teaspoon crushed fennel seeds
2 tablespoons low-fat yoghourt
juice of ½ lemon

Peel the onions and blanch for 2 minutes in boiling water. Prepare the kidneys as directed on page 118, skewering them lengthways to prevent them from curling or losing their shape. On each kebab stick allow 2 whole kidneys and surround the kidney with an onion and mushroom alternately. Mix the ingredients for the marinade and paint over the kebabs with a pastry brush. Leave in a flat dish for one hour, basting occasionally. Cook under a pre-heated grill for about 5 minutes, turning constantly.

Chinese kidneys

The Chinese use a cleaver in the way we use a knife. It is a thoroughly versatile piece of equipment and once mastered can chop, shred, dice and slice – even the handle is used to crush peppercorns. The preparation in this recipe is most important and the kidneys are sliced into matchstick strips, thereby reducing the amount of cooking to the absolute minimum.

12 kidneys
3 celery stalks

Dressing:
1 teaspoon mustard powder
1 tablespoon soya sauce

3 tablespoons sherry
juice of ½ lemon
2 drops Tabasco sauce
125 ml (¼ pint) chicken stock
salt and pepper to taste
1 teaspoon freshly chopped parsley

Prepare the kidneys as directed on page 118 and cut with the celery into very thin strips. Heat the stock until boiling, add the kidneys and celery and simmer for one minute, separating with a wooden spoon, or ideally, a pair of chopsticks. Drain immediately. Beat all the ingredients for the dressing together and pour over the meat and sprinkle with the parsley. In keeping with the Chinese mood, serve with steamed spiced bean sprouts (page 126).

Vegetables, salads, chutneys and pickles

Cooked vegetables

Vegetables when properly cooked are an essential part of a well-balanced healthy diet. In an effort to combat the sharp rise in food prices, more and more people have started to grow their own. Not only is it cheaper and satisfying, but you are guaranteed freshness and choice. However, although we may dig up our lawns or tend allotments and produce good vegetables, we fail miserably when it comes to cooking them. Overcooked, soggy vegetables are a sad, but true joke of English cookery. They should be lightly cooked and served immediately. Instead we boil them for hours and keep them warm in the oven thus reducing them to an unpalatable pulp and losing all their flavour, goodness and nourishment.

We certainly have a much wider choice of vegetables now. Until a few years ago, aubergines, courgettes, okra and bean sprouts were virtually unheard of; but we still have not yet learnt to cook them properly.

Vegetables need a relatively short time for cooking. If you like them crisp, all they need is a few minutes' poaching in lightly salted water or stock. Steaming vegetables retains their goodness and colour; roasting, braising or baking gives them a wholesome flavour which is well worth trying.

Always choose your vegetables carefully and whenever possible buy vegetables which are in season. Never buy tired or badly bruised vegetables, even if they are being sold off cheaply. They may appear to be a bargain, but I have never found that one ends up saving any money. In most cases, try to avoid peeling fresh vegetables. The skins hold most of their goodness and if they are well washed and scrubbed, there is no need to peel them. But remember that any peel, trimmings and cooking water can be added to the stockpot.

Baked vegetables

Instead of baking or roasting vegetables in the fatty dripping from a joint, try a well-flavoured tomato juice instead.

4 medium onions, *or* other root vegetables
1 clove garlic, crushed
1 teaspoon oregano
1 bay leaf

pinch of cinnamon
1 teaspoon tomato purée
½ glass red wine
125 ml (¼ pint) tomato juice
salt and pepper to taste

Peel the onions or other vegetables and cut into quarters. Mix the tomato juice with the tomato purée and wine and add the oregano and cinnamon. Put the vegetables in a baking-dish with the garlic and bay leaf and pour over the prepared tomato juice. Add salt and pepper to taste. Bake in a fairly hot oven, Gas Mark 5, 375°F, 190°C, for about 45 minutes or until cooked.

Note This recipe can be adapted to suit any root vegetable.

Baked stuffed tomatoes

6-8 ripe tomatoes
100 g (4 oz) mushrooms, finely chopped
2 celery stalks, finely chopped

½ teaspoon basil
½ teaspoon mixed herbs
salt and pepper to taste

Wash the tomatoes, cut off their tops. Carefully scoop out the insides without breaking the skin. Press the pulp through a sieve and mix with mushrooms, celery, herbs, salt and pepper. Fill the tomatoes with the mixture and replace their tops. Arrange the tomatoes in an ovenproof dish and bake in a moderate oven, Gas Mark 4, 350°F, 180°C, for about 10-15 minutes depending on their sizes.

Baked vegetables stuffed with lamb

Vegetables stuffed with a spiced meat filling are a Mediterranean dish. Courgettes, aubergines, and green peppers are most commonly used and the vegetables can either be cooked separately or as a mixture of all three. Recipes will be found on pages 108-109.

Ratatouille

This Mediterranean dish is a superb mixture of vegetables slowly stewed over a low heat. Usually cooked with oil, I have substituted tomato juice for a richer, cleaner flavour.

450 g (1 lb) tomatoes	1 teaspoon marjoram
450 g (1 lb) onions	1 teaspoon thyme
2 aubergines	1 teaspoon oregano
2 green peppers	250 ml ($\frac{1}{2}$ pint) tomato juice
2 cloves garlic	salt and pepper to taste

Cut the aubergines into thick slices and sprinkle with salt. Leave to stand in a colander with a weight on top for half an hour so that the bitter juices drain away. Wash and pat dry. Meanwhile, slice the onion and garlic, quarter the tomatoes, and remove the seeds from the green peppers and cut into rings.

Heat a little tomato juice in a heavy-based, enamelled pan and sweat the onions and garlic for a few minutes with the herbs. Add the aubergines and more tomato juice as necessary. Cook for about 10 minutes, stirring gently so that the aubergines do not break up. Add the peppers and cook for a further 10 minutes. Finally, stir in the tomatoes, and leave the vegetables to cook together until they are quite tender, adding more tomato juice if it is required. Adjust the seasoning and serve either hot or cold.

Vegetable purées

Many of us dismiss vegetable purées as mere babies' food or invalid pap; but light and airy with a creamy velvet texture they are delicious served with meat or fish. In addition to the two recipes suggested, I particularly recommend carrots blended with a dash of dry vermouth and chives or Jerusalem artichokes with a pinch of chervil.

Parsnip purée

Parsnips have just the right texture to purée. Tournefort wrote in *The Compleat Herbal* (1730) that they were best eaten at the time of Lent 'for that they are the sweatest, by reason the juice has been concocted during the winter, and are desired at that season especially, both for their agreeable Taste and their Wholesomeness. For they are not so good in any respect, till they have been first nipt with Cold.'

450 g (1 lb) parsnips	salt and freshly ground black
1 small carton cultured buttermilk	pepper

Peel the parsnips and cook in lightly salted boiling water until tender. Strain and purée in a blender or pass through a sieve or vegetable mouli. Stir in the buttermilk until it forms the consistency of a smooth paste; the purée should be creamy but not too runny. Add salt and freshly ground black pepper to taste.

Spinach purée

1 kg (2 lb) spinach	1 carton cultured buttermilk
pinch of nutmeg	salt and pepper to taste
juice of half an orange	

Wash the spinach thoroughly in cold water and throw away any of the stringy stalks. Tear the leaves into smallish pieces and put into a saucepan with just enough water to prevent the spinach from sticking to the bottom of the pan. Add salt, cover and simmer over a gentle heat until it has reduced to a pulp. Strain thoroughly, pressing the leaves so that any excess liquid drains away. Liquidize in a blender, adding the buttermilk slowly to prevent it from curdling. Add the nutmeg and orange juice and adjust the seasoning. Heat in a warm oven before serving.

Steamed vegetables

Vegetables should be steamed over a flavoured liquid – chicken or vegetable stock or a lightly flavoured water. They must not be overcooked as the whole point of steaming is to allow them to absorb the seasoning while retaining a crisp, crunchy texture. If you intend to steam cook often, it is probably worth your while investing in a proper steamer (see notes on equipment on page 15). Otherwise you can improvise with a colander or plate suspended over a half-filled saucepan.

Steamed broccoli

450 g (1 lb) broccoli
pinch of sesame seeds

juice of half a lemon
salt to taste

Wash and trim the broccoli and break into spears. Arrange in steamer and sprinkle with sesame seeds. Add salt to taste and pour over lemon juice. Steam until tender.

Steamed vegetable marrow

1 small vegetable marrow
1 small piece fresh ginger

salt to taste

Peel the marrow and scoop out the seeds. Cut into 1-inch thick slices. Peel and crush the ginger with a little salt. Arrange the marrow with the ginger on the steamer and steam until tender.

Spiced steamed bean sprouts

450 g (1 lb) bean sprouts
1 spring onion, chopped
¼ teaspoon ground ginger

2 tablespoons soya sauce
salt to taste

Wash the bean sprouts and drain thoroughly. Arrange on the steamer. Sprinkle with the spring onion, ground ginger and the soya sauce. Steam until tender.

Note   If fresh bean sprouts are not available, use a tin instead.

Braised vegetables

The principle of braising vegetables is to cook them slowly in a little liquid either over a low heat on top of the oven or in a slow oven. The vegetables can be braised in a brick – preferably not a fish brick as the strong flavour of the fish would drown the taste – or in an earthenware or cast-iron casserole or in an ovenproof dish. Cooking times will depend on your taste, but I think as a general rule we all tend to overcook and spoil our vegetables, so allow less time than you think. Celery, cabbage, turnips and onions can all be successfully braised.

Braised mixed vegetables

4 medium carrots
2 leeks
2 medium onions
2-3 celery stalks

1 turnip
½ teaspoon mixed herbs
125 ml (¼ pint) well-flavoured
  stock

Wash and scrub the vegetables. Quarter the onions and cut the remaining vegetables into 3-inch strips. Put in a dish or saucepan and almost cover with stock. Add the mixed herbs and either bake in a warm oven, Gas Mark 3, 325°F, 170°C, or simmer covered on a very low heat for about half an hour

Note   Since the advent of North Sea gas it is sometimes difficult to control heat for a low simmer without the flame going out. If this is the case, use a heat-diffusing mat between the heat source and the saucepan – it will solve all your problems.

Braised Brussels sprouts in wine

450 g (1 lb) Brussels sprouts
2 spring onions, sliced
1 clove garlic, sliced
pinch of nutmeg

½ teaspoon cumin seeds
1 glass dry white wine
125 ml (¼ pint) chicken stock
salt and pepper to taste

Wash and trim the Brussels sprouts. Put in a dish or saucepan with the onions and garlic and add the cumin seeds and nutmeg. Pour over the white wine and chicken stock and bake in a slow oven, Gas Mark 2, 300°F, 150°C, or simmer covered for about 20 minutes, until tender.

Braised chicory

675 g (1½ lb) chicory
½ teaspoon lemon thyme
juice of half a lemon

375 ml (¾ pint) chicken stock
salt and pepper to taste

Wash the chicory and split in half down the middle. Lay the pieces flat in a baking-dish, add the lemon thyme, salt and pepper to taste and pour over the lemon juice and chicken stock. Cover and bake in a moderate oven, Gas Mark 4, 350°F, 180°C, for about 20 minutes or until tender.

Braised cabbage with juniper berries

The Italians blanch cabbage in boiling salted water before braising. It helps to retain the taste and texture.

1 large white cabbage
4-6 juniper berries
1 tablespoon wine vinegar

250 ml (½ pint) chicken stock
salt and cayenne pepper to taste

Cut the cabbage into quarters and remove the stalk. Shred it coarsely. Blanch in boiling salted water for 5 minutes. Drain and wash in cold water to refresh it. Arrange the cabbage with the

juniper berries in a pan and pour over the vinegar and chicken
stock. Cover and simmer, or bake in a slow oven, Gas Mark 2,
300°F, 150°C, until cooked. Serve garnished with cayenne
pepper.

Vegetable sauces

'Sauces are to cooking what grammar is to language.' (M Soyer.)

Vegetable sauces are one of the delights of fat-free cooking.
Light and foamy, they add an extra dimension to grilled or
roasted meat and fish. Generally the food is cooked in such a way
that the ingredients can be strained, sieved or puréed to make a
sauce of their own, but it is always useful to be able to whisk up a
separate sauce to accompany a plainly cooked meat.

None of these sauces are complicated to make, they rely on
fresh good vegetables and a well-flavoured stock, and, like all
good sauces, they should be served at the table piping hot.

Basic vegetable gravy

The principle for making a well-flavoured clear gravy is the same
for all meat, poultry and game, vary the stock and choice of
vegetables according to the dish served.

1 large carrot	1 bay leaf
1 stick celery	1 glass of wine (red or white)
1 medium onion	250 ml ($\frac{1}{2}$ pint) stock
sprig of parsley	salt and pepper to taste
$\frac{1}{2}$ teaspoon thyme	

Wash and cut the vegetables into thin strips about 1-inch thick.
Heat a little stock in a saucepan and cook all the vegetables,
stirring constantly, for a few minutes. Add the rest of the stock
and simmer until the stock is well flavoured. Strain through a
sieve, pressing the vegetables with a wooden spoon so that all the
flavour is extracted. Return the stock to the pan and add the glass of
wine. Bring to the boil and simmer for a few minutes. Adjust the

seasoning and serve piping hot.

Note If the gravy is too watery, reduce it by boiling rapidly for a few minutes after the wine has been added.

Sauce for freshwater fish

It is interesting that this recipe for a sauce to serve with grilled or baked fish was written in 1893 – long before fat-free cooking was ever thought about. 'Mince half a dozen mushrooms, half a dozen onions, and half a clove of garlic. Put the vegetables into a saucepan, pour over them as much stock as will cover them, and simmer gently till the sauce is pleasantly flavoured. Strain the liquor through a jelly bag, and press with the back of a wooden spoon to obtain as much sauce as possible. Add a glass of claret, boil up once more and serve. A few drops of anchovy essence may be added or not, as preferred.' (Cassell's *Dictionary of Cookery,* London 1893.)

Note Use a well-flavoured fish stock (page 26).

Cucumber sauce

Made with fish stock, this sauce makes a great accompaniment to steamed or poached fish. However you can substitute chicken for fish stock and serve it with chicken instead.

1 small cucumber	100 g (4 oz) cottage cheese
250 ml (½ pint) fish or chicken stock	½ teaspoon dill
½ glass white wine	salt and pepper to taste

Peel and finely slice the cucumber. Poach the slices in the stock of your choice with the white wine until they are quite tender. Allow the liquid to cool slightly before liquidizing. Add the cottage cheese and dill to the cucumber and blend thoroughly to a smooth consistency. Season to taste. If you want to re-heat the sauce use a double boiler to prevent it from curdling.

Spinach sauce

225 g (8 oz) fresh spinach   1 dessertspoon stock
pinch of nutmeg   salt and pepper to taste
2 tablespoons *fromage blanc* (p.20)

Wash the spinach thoroughly and discard any stringy stalks. Put
into a saucepan with just enough water to prevent it sticking to
the bottom of the pan. Cover and simmer over a gentle heat until
it is cooked. Strain and squeeze dry by pressing it against the
sides of the sieve with a wooden spoon. Put the spinach in a
liquidizer with the stock, nutmeg, and *fromage blanc*. Blend until
smooth. Adjust the seasoning and keep warm in a double
saucepan until required. Serve with either fish or white meat.

Fresh tomato sauce

The Italians cook their sweet, ripe tomatoes with plenty of sweet
basil – the taste is superb. Depending on how they want to use the
sauce they either serve it quite liquid or leave it to stew for hours
until it reduces to a rich-wine pulp. If you make a large quantity
either freeze it or store it in the fridge and use instead of tomato
juice or purée.

1 kg (2 lb) tomatoes $\frac{1}{2}$ teaspoon mixed herbs
1 large onion, chopped   1 bay leaf
2 cloves garlic, chopped   salt and pepper to taste
1 teaspoon basil

Scald the tomatoes in boiling water until their skins are loosened.
Peel and roughly chop, making sure that you retain all their juice.
Put the tomatoes in a pan with the juice, onions, garlic and herbs.
Add the salt and pepper, cover and simmer gently over a very low
heat, stirring occasionally until it has reached the required
consistency. Liquidize and serve.

Note The tomatoes can also be baked in a slow oven, Gas Mark
2, 300°F, 150°C. In this case it is not necessary to peel them first,
just cut them in half, sprinkle the tops with the herbs and bake
uncovered for about half an hour. Pass the pulp through a sieve
before serving.

Salads and dressings

A true lover of salads knows that virtually any ingredients can be incorporated into a salad. Proust wrote once of eating a confection of pineapple and truffles; nowadays our tastes tend to be a little less exotic!

There are many kinds of salads – vegetables, fruit, cheese, fish and meat – and the best known is the green salad. I was once told that a test of a good cook lies in a satisfying salad. If the standard of most green salads is anything to go by, most of us would fail dismally. Those endless plates of limp lettuce, garnished with a slice of cucumber and the occasional sprig of mustard and cress are enough to make anyone recoil with horror.

A good green salad is a rare treat. There is a wide choice of lettuces – cabbage, cos, Iceberg and Webb's Wonder are the best known – and if eaten when fresh, they are sweet tasting and crisply textured. Like the French, who are justly famous for their green salads, throw in a few chopped herbs, a shredded green pepper, a few slices of chicory or endive and even a handful of freshly picked dandelion leaves. In fact almost anything as long as it is green.

Salads are versatile, they can be served as hors-d'oeuvre – sliced tomatoes sprinkled with herbs – or as an accompaniment to the main course or as a complete meal in themselves. A bowl piled high with fresh sliced vegetables, mixed with diced cold chicken and garnished with hard-boiled eggs is all you need on a warm day. Most vegetables make a satisfying salad – raw mushrooms, shredded cabbage, grated carrots and marinated leeks are but a few examples – and when lettuces are scarce, have a French bean or raw spinach salad instead.

There are no rules to salad making, you can make a salad out of whatever ingredients you choose; but there are a few important points to remember. Always use fresh vegetables, a limp lettuce makes a limp salad and the texture of the salad is vital. Wash and trim your vegetables and dry them thoroughly before use. It is not necessary to peel all the vegetables (I prefer cucumber left unpeeled and it is less trouble), but make sure that you remove all the strings from vegetables like French beans, mange-tout and celery. If you use raw onions in a salad it is advisable to blanch them for a few minutes in boiling water to remove some of their strong taste as they can be a little harsh. Unless the recipe specifically states that the ingredients should be marinaded, do not dress the salad hours before serving, it will go soggy. Prepare the dressing and pour it over the salad, giving it a good toss to coat all the leaves. If possible use fresh herbs, otherwise soften dried herbs in a little fresh lemon juice, before adding them to the dressing.

The dressing is the salad's crowning touch. For a fat-free dressing, yoghourt or buttermilk (instead of oil), mustard and lemon juice or vinegar are essential ingredients.

Basic salad dressing 1:
fresh herbs of choice
½ teaspoon mustard
2 tablespoons cultured buttermilk
1 teaspoon vinegar (see note below)
salt and pepper to taste

Basic salad dressing 2:
fresh herbs of choice
½ teaspoon mustard
2 tablespoons low-fat yoghourt
juice of half a lemon
salt and pepper to taste

Basic sald dressing 3:
fresh herbs of choice
½ teaspoon mustard
2 tablespoons cottage cheese, sieved
juice of half a lemon
salt and pepper to taste

Mix all the ingredients for the dressing of your choice together and chill before pouring over the salad.

The flavours can be varied by using different herbs or adding a crushed clove of garlic, a minced onion, 2 or 3 chopped spring onions, a yolk of a hard-boiled egg or a teaspoon of chopped capers. It is important to use a good mustard: I like a strong Dijon or Moutarde de Meaux or one of the Maille herbal mustards which come in a range of flavours including tarragon, basil or green peppercorn. However if it is a sharper taste you are after, nothing beats Colman's English mustard.

Note Use a flavoured vinegar for the dressing. They are simple to make. All you need is a glass bottle with a tightly fitting lid or stopper, a sprig of fresh herbs and a good-quality vinegar. Put the herbs of your choice – tarragon, rosemary or mint – in the bottle and add the vinegar. Seal and leave to infuse for at least 2 weeks before use. Garlic vinegar is made in exactly the same way using 1 or 2 peeled fresh cloves of garlic.

Egg sauce

I have read that liquid paraffin is allowed in fat-free cooking as, to put it bluntly, its advantage over other oil is that it passes straight through your body. I find the idea so off-putting that I would rather go without it all together. Instead I make a light creamy egg sauce which in colour and texture is rather similar to mayonnaise and is delicious served with salad.

1 egg yolk	5-6 tablespoons well-flavoured
dash of lemon juice	stock
	salt and pepper to taste

For this recipe you need a double boiler. If you do not have one, improvise by resting a heatproof mixing bowl in a saucepan half filled with water. Make sure that it is a tight fit, otherwise you will have trouble gripping it when you beat the egg yolk.

Break the yolk into the bowl and add a dash of lemon juice. Beat the two together with a wire whisk and place in a saucepan of boiling water. As you continue to beat, the yolk will start to thicken. Slowly add the stock, beating constantly so that it is incorporated with the yolk. If you add the stock too quickly the sauce will not set and will separate. This can be adjusted once the sauce is removed from the heat, by whisking in a little softened gelatine and chilling in the fridge. If the consistency of the sauce is too thick to pour over a salad, thin it down by beating in a little buttermilk.

Suggested variations

Lemon sauce: Use a lightly flavoured chicken stock with the grated rind from a lemon and a pinch of lemon balm.

Creamed egg sauce: When the sauce has set, stir in about 2 tablespoons of *fromage blanc* (page 20) or 50-75 g (2-3 oz) of sieved cottage cheese.

Herb sauce: Chop a selection of fresh herbs, tarragon, thyme, oregano, marjoram and stir into the sauce once it has set.

Seafood sauce: Mix the sauce with a crushed clove of garlic and 2 tablespoons of well-seasoned tomato juice.

Fennel and lemon salad

1 head of fennel
Dressing
1 tablespoon chopped parsley

grated rind and juice of 1 lemon
1 carton low-fat yoghourt
salt and pepper to taste

Wash the fennel and cut into slices about 1-inch thick. Blanch in boiling water for about 1 minute, drain and refresh. Mix all the ingredients for the dressing and pour over the fennel. Chill thoroughly before serving.

Cucumber with honey dressing

1 cucumber
1 teaspoon dill weed, chopped
salt

Dressing:
2 teaspoons honey
2 tablespoons vinegar

Peel and thinly slice the cucumber. Sprinkle with dill and salt and leave to drain. Heat the honey in a saucepan and as it begins to melt, add the vinegar. Remove from the heat and allow to cool before pouring the dressing over the cucumber.

Carrot salad

450 g (1 lb) carrots
1 medium onion, minced
2 juniper berries, crushed
1 bay leaf

2 tablespoons herb vinegar (p.132)
salt to taste
water

Peel and coarsely grate the carrots. Put the carrots in a saucepan with the juniper berries, bay leaf, vinegar and enough water to cover. Bring to the boil and boil fiercely until almost all the liquid has evaporated and the carrots are tender. Add the salt and leave to cool before serving.

Beetroot and cardamom salad

Beetroots can be bought cooked or raw. Ideally it is better to cook them yourself and add the dressing while they are still warm.

3 large beetroots	1 tablespoon white wine vinegar
Dressing	salt and freshly ground black
6-8 cardamom pods	pepper
2 tablespoons low-fat yoghourt	

Wrap the beetroots in greasproof paper and bake in a slow oven, Gas Mark 2, 300°F, 150°C, for about 3 hours. When they are cooked the skin will easily rub off. Peel and cut into thin slices and arrange in a dish. Crush the cardamom pods to release the seeds and pound the seeds in a pestle and mortar. Mix the cardamom seeds with the remaining ingredients for the dressing and pour over the beetroot. Chill thoroughly before serving.

Note Beetroots can also be boiled in a little water but great care should be taken when cleaning not to break the skins as the beetroots will lose their colour.

French bean salad

450 g (1 lb) French beans	chopped parsley
1 small onion	salt
3-4 tablespoons basic dressing (p.132)	

Top and tail the beans and boil in lightly salted water for 10-15 minutes. Drain and leave to cool. Blanch the whole onion in boiling water for a few minutes and drain. Mince the onion and mix with the beans. Pour the dressing over the salad and chill in the fridge for about an hour before serving. Garnish with plenty of chopped parsley.

Note You can add one or two slices of diced ham to make it a more substantial dish.

Cauliflower salad

1 firm white cauliflower	3-4 tablespoons basic dressing (p.132)
2 tomatoes, sliced	salt
1 teaspoon thyme	

Wash and trim the cauliflower and break into florets. Cook in lightly salted water for about 5 minutes. Drain and mix with the dressing while still warm. Chill and add the tomatoes just before serving.

Tarragon chicken and orange salad

100 g (4 oz) cooked chicken, diced
2 large oranges, peeled and sliced
1 head of lettuce
grated peel of 1 orange

½ teaspoon tarragon
2-3 tablespoons egg sauce (p.133)
salt and pepper to taste

Mix the chicken with the egg sauce, tarragon and grated orange peel. Wash and shred the lettuce and arrange in a bowl. Alternate with a layer of orange slices and a layer of chicken. Garnish with an extra sprig of tarragon and serve chilled.

Chutneys and pickles

Nothing beats a home-made chutney or pickle. The satisfaction of opening a store cupboard crammed full of clearly labelled shining jars is well worth the initial effort. Chutneys and pickles are best made towards the end of summer when vegetables are at their cheapest and most plentiful. Always choose fresh, firm, unblemished vegetables and wash them thoroughly before use. The spices should be as fresh as possible and it helps to use good-quality vinegar, otherwise the flavour is too harsh. Store in sterilized, airtight jars; preparations with vinegar have a tendency to dry out so you must make sure that they are well sealed.

Pickled cauliflower and red cabbage

This is a Middle Eastern pickle which I first ate when I was in Beirut. I was delighted to find the recipe in Claudia Roden's *A Book of Middle Eastern Food,* and so with her permission I quote her version.

1 young white cauliflower
½ red or white cabbage
4-5 level tablespoons (about 75 g (3 oz) salt

250 ml (½ pint) white wine vinegar
1 small dried chilli pepper pod (optional)
750 ml (1½ pints) water

Wash the cauliflower and separate into little florets. Cut the cabbage into thick slices in one direction, and then again thickly in the other direction. Leave it in chunks; do not shred it or take the leaves apart. Pack into a large glass jar, arranging alternate layers of cauliflower and cabbage chunks.

Mix salt, water and vinegar in a glass or china container. Pour the liquid over the vegetables, and bury a chilli pod in the jar if you like. Close tightly, with a glass top if possible, and store in a warm place for about 10 days, by which time the vegetables will be mellow and ready to eat.

Note If using white cabbage, colour the pickle with a few slices of raw beetroot.

Onion and marrow pickle

1 small marrow
225 g (8 oz) small pickling onions
2 fresh chillies, chopped
6 g (¼ oz) ginger, ground
6 g (¼ oz) turmeric

1 teaspoon honey
750 ml (1½ pints) white wine vinegar
12 g (½ oz) salt

Peel the marrow and scoop out the seeds and pith. Cut the marrow into small cubes and lay out on a flat dish. Sprinkle with salt and leave to stand for about 6 hours or overnight. Rinse and drain the marrow and pat dry with a kitchen cloth. Pour the vinegar into a preserving-pan with the spices and simmer for about half an hour. Add the marrow and onions and simmer, stirring carefully so as not to break the marrow. Leave to cook until it starts to thicken. Add the honey and boil for a further 5 minutes, stirring so that it does not stick to the bottom of the pan. Pour into sterilized jars and seal. Leave for a good 2 months before opening.

Tomato and green pepper chutney

1 kg (2½ lb) ripe tomatoes
2 large green peppers
2 large onions, chopped
1 clove garlic, crushed
25 g (1 oz) fresh ginger root,
  peeled and crushed
6 g (¼ oz) celery seed
6 g (¼ oz) mustard seed

2-3 cloves
2-3 cumin seeds
6 peppercorns
6 g (¼ oz) salt
1 bay leaf
1 teaspoon molasses
375 ml (¾ pint) white wine vinegar

Scald the tomatoes in boiling water until their skins are loosened. Peel, cut into halves and remove the pips and fleshy core. Pass them through a sieve to extract the juice. Blanch the green peppers in hot water and refresh. Cut into thin slices and discard the seeds. Put the tomatoes with the juice into a pan with the peppers and onions, garlic, bay leaf, peppercorns, molasses and salt. Simmer gently for about 20 minutes. Meanwhile, bring to the boil the vinegar with all the remaining spices. Cover and simmer for about 5 minutes to allow the spices to infuse their flavour. Strain and add the vinegar to the tomatoes. Stir the ingredients together and simmer gently until the chutney thickens, and add more salt if required. Bottle into sterilized jars and seal tightly immediately. Leave a good 6 weeks before eating.

Eastern chutney

Most apple-based chutneys use only cooking apples. If, like me, you have a slightly sweet tooth, I would advise you to make this recipe with equal quantities of eating and cooking apples; otherwise you may find the flavour a little tart.

675 g (1½ lb) cooking apples, *or*
  325 g (12 oz) eating apples and
  325 g (12 oz) cooking apples
50 g (2 oz) seedless raisins
2 cloves garlic, crushed
50 g (2 oz) fresh root ginger,
  peeled and grated

50 g (2 oz) chillies, chopped
100 g (4 oz) mustard seed
1 teaspoon molasses
750 ml (1½ pints) white wine
  vinegar
100 g (4 oz) salt
250 ml (½ pint) water

Peel and core the apples and roughly chop. Simmer the apples in the water in a preserving-pan or a large saucepan until soft, stirring constantly so that they do not burn. Remove from the heat and stir in the prepared garlic, spices and salt, raisins and molasses. Return to the heat and slowly bring to the boil. When it is bubbling, reduce the heat and simmer for a further 10 minutes. Bottle immediately into sterilized jars. Leave to cool before sealing tightly.

Pickled cucumber

1 kg (2 lb) small ridge cucumbers
1 teaspoon dill seed
1 teaspoon dill weed, chopped
6-8 peppercorns

325 ml ($\frac{3}{4}$ pint) white vinegar
water
salt

Wash the cucumbers and pat dry. Prick them all over with a fork and soak for 24 hours in a solution of 1 teaspoon of salt to every pint of water used. Rinse the cucumbers, drain thoroughly and pack tightly into sterilized jars. Add the dill weed and peppercorns to the jars. Meanwhile, bring the vinegar to the boil with an equal amount of water and about 2 tablespoons of salt. Add the dill seed and simmer for a few minutes. Pour the liquid over the cucumbers. Seal the jars and store in a cool place. Leave for a few days before eating.

The pudding course

Eliza Acton in *Modern Cookery for Private Families*, 1845, is sensible enough to point out that 'For common occasions, a few dishes of really fresh fruit, tastefully disposed and embedded in large green leaves, will be all that is required for a plain summer or autumn dessert.' For special occasions, however, 'A well selected and well arranged dessert, however simple in its character, may always be rendered agreeable to the eye and to the taste.'

I have included a few simple recipes for various puddings which are easy to prepare but which will add the crowning touch to a satisfying meal. Try to use fruit that is in season. It is less extravagant and a way of ensuring better quality and sweeter taste. If the fruit is to be cooked or marinaded, it is advisable to choose it slightly under-ripe, in this way you will avoid it going too soft. To prevent the fruit from discolouring, once it has been peeled, either store it tightly covered in a fridge or soak it in a little lemon juice. To sweeten the ingredients, use melted honey, cinnamon, nutmeg or orange juice. Certain herbs, angelica, elderflower and sweet cicely, take away the tartness from fruit, so add a pinch when stewing. Desserts, as Eliza Acton says, 'should be rendered agreeable to the eye' and they can be served in individual ramekins, little glass dishes, moulded and turned out on to an attractive plate, or to quote Miss Acton yet again, 'may be served in any kind of style'.

Stewed rhubarb with angelica

Mrs M Grieve in *The Modern Herbal* writes, 'If a small quantity of the leaf stalk of Angelica be cooked with 'sticks' of rhubarb, the flavour of the compound will be acceptable to many who do not relish plain rhubarb.'

If possible use fresh angelica; otherwise dried angelica, not to be confused with candied angelica, can be bought from good herbalists and health food shops.

450 g (1 lb) rhubarb
1 teaspoon angelica
juice and grated rind of 1 orange

1 teaspoon honey
water

Wash and trim the rhubarb, discarding the leaves and the upper ends of the stalks and cut into small pieces. Put the rhubarb in a saucepan with the angelica, orange juice and peel, honey and enough water to cover. Slowly bring to the boil, cover and simmer until tender. Serve either hot or cold.

Stewed rhubarb with ginger

An alternative recipe for rhubarb is to cook it with sweet cicely, ground ginger and lemon juice.

450 g (1 lb) rhubarb
1 teaspoon sweet cicely
pinch of ground ginger
juice and grated rind of 1 lemon

juice and grated rind of 1 orange
1 teaspoon honey
water

Prepare the rhubarb as in the previous recipe. Put in a saucepan with all the ingredients and sufficient water to cover, slowly bring to the boil, cover and simmer until tender.

Note Rhubarb can also be baked in a covered dish in a warm oven, Gas Mark 3, 325°F, 170°C.

Stuffed apples

Baked apples remind me of my childhood. Apples crammed with nuts and raisins and dripping with honey were a special treat reserved for high days, holidays and when my sisters and I had been particularly well-behaved! To this day they are still one of my favourite puddings.

4-6 cooking apples
50 g (2 oz) chopped nuts
50 g (2 oz) seedless raisins

1 teaspoon cinnamon
2 tablespoons honey

Wash the apples and dry thoroughly. Run the blade of a sharp knife lightly round the skin to prevent it from splitting while cooking. Cut out the core with a fruit corer and hollow out the centre of the apples. Mix the nuts, raisins and cinnamon with 1 tablespoon honey and spoon the mixture into the hollowed-out centres. Place the apples in a shallow ovenproof dish and dribble the remainder of the honey on top. Bake in a moderate oven, Gas Mark 4, 350°F, 180°C, until tender.

Apple fluff

Use eating apples rather than cooking apples for this recipe as they make a sweeter, refreshingly light pudding.

675 g (1½ lb) apples (Golden Delicious, Russets, etc)
2-3 cloves
juice of half a lemon

100 g (4 oz) cottage cheese
1 tablespoon cultured buttermilk
2 egg whites
water

Peel and core the apples and cut into quarters. Cook on a low heat with the cloves and lemon juice and sufficient water to prevent the apples from burning the bottom of the saucepan. When the apples are soft, pass through a sieve and leave to cool. Sieve the cottage cheese and add to the apples with the butter-milk or liquidize in a blender if preferred. Beat the egg whites until stiff and carefully fold into the apples. Leave to chill thoroughly before serving.

Lemon soufflé

Cold soufflés are particularly appealing, for although they are not cooked they are dressed to look as if they have risen above the dish.

juice and grated rind of 3 lemons
pinch of cinnamon
1 tablespoon clear honey
3 eggs, separated

1 carton low-fat yoghourt
3 teaspoons powdered gelatine
water

To prepare the soufflé dish, tie a band of greaseproof paper around the outside of the dish, to stand about 2 inches above the rim to support the mixture as its sets. Mix the lemon juice and rind with the cinnamon and honey in a bowl. Place the bowl over a saucepan half-filled with water. Beat the egg yolks and stir into the mixture. Continue stirring until the mixture starts to thicken and remove from the heat. Whip the yoghourt until smooth and pour it in with the lemons. Dissolve the gelatine in a little hot water and add to the mixture. Whisk the egg whites until stiff and fold in carefully with a metal spoon. Pour the mixture into the prepared soufflé dish. Chill until set. To remove the greaseproof paper, dip a palette knife into hot water and run it between the edge of the soufflé and the paper so that it can easily be peeled off.

Gooseberry soufflé

In the country it is said that summer has not truly arrived until the elder is fully in flower. The flowers are often used in cooking; sweet scented with a cooling taste, they are beaten into batters to lighten the texture, and in Victorian times, were always added to the christening posset to bless and protect the new-born child.

450 g (1 lb) gooseberries
4-5 heads of elderflowers
1 teaspoon honey
3 eggs, separated

1 carton low-fat yoghourt
3 teaspoons powdered gelatine
water

Prepare the soufflé dish as in the recipe for Lemon Soufflé (above). Top and tail the gooseberries. Tie the elderflowers in a piece of muslin and put them in a saucepan with the gooseberries, honey and a little water. Cook on a low heat until soft. Remove the elderflowers and pass the fruit through a sieve to make a purée. Place the bowl over a saucepan half filled with water and continue beating until the mixture starts to thicken, remove from the heat and whip the yoghourt until smooth; dissolve the gelatine in a little hot water and add both to the purée. Whisk the egg whites until stiff and fold carefully into the fruit with a metal spoon. Pour into the prepared soufflé dish and leave to set.

To remove the greaseproof paper dip a palette knife into hot water and run it between the edge of the soufflé and the paper so that it can be peeled off easily.

Blackberry 'junket'

Late summer is blackberry time. There is an abundance of wild blackberries in the woods, heaths and commons – enough for all of us to pick. We all have our favourite blackberry recipes and I particularly like Richard Mabey's from his interesting and useful book *Food for Free*, which is a 'junket' made from nothing other than blackberry juice. Served with plain yoghourt it is delicious.

'Remove the juice from the very ripest berries with the help of a juice extractor, or by pressing through several layers of muslin. Then simply allow the thick, dark juice to stand undisturbed in a warm room. Do not stir or cool the juice, or add anything to it. In a few hours it will have set to the consistency of a light junket.'

Blackberry and apple mousse

If you use sweet eating apples instead of tart cookers, it should not be necessary to add any sugar to this recipe.

450 g (1 lb) ripe blackberries
3 eating apples (Cox, Golden Delicious)
juice of half a lemon
2 egg whites
3 teaspoons powdered gelatine
water

Wash the blackberries and drain thoroughly. Peel, core and slice the apples and cook with the berries in a little water until soft. Purée the fruit through a sieve and leave to cool. Dissolve the gelatine in a little hot water, add the lemon juice, and stir in with the fruit. Whisk the egg whites until stiff and carefully fold into the mixture. Pour into a mould and chill until set.

Raspberry mousse

450 g (1 lb) fresh raspberries
2 egg whites
100 g (4 oz) *fromage blanc* (p.20)
2 tablespoons low-fat yoghourt
3 teaspoons powdered gelatine
water

Wash the raspberries and purée by passing through a sieve. Beat the *fromage blanc* with the yoghourt until smooth and fold into the purée. Dissolve the gelatine in a little hot water and add to the mixture. Whip the egg whites until stiff and fold into the purée. Chill until set.

Note Fresh ripe raspberries are generally sweet enough without any added sugar. However, if you find the flavour a little tart, add a dash of orange juice or a teaspoon of honey melted in a little water.

Stewed pears with cardamom

There are 150 different varieties of pears. Conference is the most widely grown in Britain, whereas William's Bon Chretien, juicy with a rich muscatel flavour is the best-known pear of all. Stewing pears like Bellisime d'Hiver and Pitmaston Duchess tend to be hard and lacking in flavour and need slow cooking in a flavoured syrup. Any pear can be stewed but make sure that it is firm and slightly under-ripe.

6 firm pears
4-6 cardamom pods

1 tablespoon honey
1 glass red wine

Peel the pears, cut into halves lengthways and remove the core. Lay them flat in a shallow ovenproof dish. Crush the cardamom pods to release the seeds. Heat the red wine with the cardamom seeds in a saucepan and add the honey, stirring continuously until it melts. Pour the wine into the hollow of each pear and over the top. Cover the dish and bake in a moderate oven, Gas Mark 4, 350°F, 180°C, until tender. Leave to cool before serving.

Note An alternative recipe is to cook the pears in exactly the same way but to substitute a tablespoon of carob powder for the cardamoms.

Plum and pear jam

This is a delicious jam which needs absolutely no sugar or sweetener and is set by the high content of pectin in the plums. It can be eaten like a conserve, with a spoon, or as an ordinary jam.

1 kg (2 lb) ripe plums	stick of cinnamon, crushed
1 kg (2 lb) firm pears	4-5 cloves
juice and grated rind of 2 lemons	teacup of water

Peel, core and roughly chop the pears, leave them to soak in a bowl with the lemon juice and peel. Meanwhile, stone the plums and cut into halves. Cook them in a preserving-pan over a low heat with the cinnamon, cloves and water. Stir the plums frequently until soft. Add the pears with the lemons to the pan and cook the fruit for a further hour, adding some more water should it be necessary to prevent the fruit from sticking to the bottom of the pan. When the fruit has been reduced to a pulp, pass through a sieve. Bottle in sterilized jars and store in a cool place.

Pears in red wine jelly

4 large pears	juice of half a lemon
pinch of grated nutmeg	250 ml (½ pint) red wine
1 teaspoon cinnamon	3 teaspoons powdered gelatine
2 cloves	water

Peel and core the pears. Cut into small slices and soak in the lemon juice. Heat the wine in a saucepan with the spices until almost boiling. Add the pears, cover and simmer until tender. Strain the pears and arrange them on the bottom of a dish. Dissolve the gelatine in a little hot water and stir in with the wine. Pour the mixture over the pears and leave in a cool place until set.

Orange and lemon cheese

450 g (1 lb) *fromage blanc* (p.20), *or* yoghourt cheese (p.21)	juice and grated rind of 1 orange
juice and grated rind of 2 lemons	1 tablespoon cultured buttermilk

Mix the *fromage blanc* with the juice and grated rind of the lemons, and the orange juice in a bowl. Beat in the buttermilk until the cheese is a smooth texture. Arrange in individual portions, chill and serve decorated with the grated orange rind.

Orange and pineapple salad

4 large oranges
1 small pineapple

1 tablespoon honey
2 tablespoons rum

Peel the oranges, cut into rings and remove the pips. Pare the rind with a potato peeler to remove the pith and cut into fine strips. Blanch the peel in boiling water, drain and refresh in cold water. Peel the pineapple and cut into rings. Arrange the oranges and pineapple in alternate layers in a bowl. Heat the rum and honey over a low heat with any orange and pineapple juice which may have been squeezed from the fruit while preparing it. Pour the liquor over the fruit and decorate the top with the peel. Chill in the fridge for 2-3 hours before serving.

Peaches in brandy

Peaches soaked in brandy have a taste of luxury. I have also tried this recipe with gin and vodka, both work equally well.

4 ripe peaches
pinch of cinnamon
grated rind of half a lemon
1 tablespoon honey

3 tablespoons brandy, *or* 3 tablespoons gin, *or* 3 tablespoons vodka

Peel the peaches, cut into thin slices and arrange in a dish. Heat the honey in a saucepan with the brandy and cinnamon until it is melted. Pour it over the peaches and decorate the top with the lemon rind. Leave to marinade in a cool place for a minimum of 12 hours before serving.

Strawberries in white wine

Strawberries in a white wine marinade have a delicious flavour. Do not wash the fruit as it make them soggy – just wipe them carefully with a damp cloth.

450 g (1 lb) strawberries
juice and grated rind of 1 orange

glass of white wine

Hull the strawberries and cut into halves. Arrange them in a bowl in layers. Mix the orange juice and white wine and pour it over the strawberries. Garnish the top with the grated peel and chill for at least 2 hours before serving.

Coffee pots de crème

2 eggs
2 tablespoons instant coffee
1 tablespoon brandy

500 ml (1 pint) milk (made up from 100 g (4 oz) low-fat skimmed milk and 500 ml (1 pint) water)

Heat the milk until almost boiling. Remove from the heat and beat in the eggs. Mix the instant coffee with the brandy and stir into the milk. Strain the mixture through a sieve and pour into individual ramekins. Place the ramekins in a baking-dish half filled with water and cover. Bake in a slow oven, Gas Mark 3, 325°F, 170°C, for 45 minutes or until the milk has set.

Ice cream, water ices and fruit ices

Ice cream, water ices and fruit ices are simple to make and do not need any special equipment – if you have an ice-cream maker it saves a certain amount of trouble but you can do perfectly well without one.

A few points to remember about making ice cream: if you need to alter the fridge control set it at freezing point and chill the utensils beforehand, it will quicken the process. Ice cream should be set quickly in the freezer or freezing compartment of the fridge or the texture will be grainy and it should be beaten to ensure that it is smooth and velvety. The flavour becomes milder as it freezes so do not worry if it should taste a little sharp at first.

Vanilla ice cream

2 eggs
1 teaspoon vanilla essence
2 teaspoons powdered gelatine
liquid artificial sweetener to taste

500 ml (1 pint) milk (made up from 50 g (2 oz) low-fat skimmed milk and 500 ml (1 pint) water)

Heat the milk until almost boiling and pour it over the eggs. Beat the milk and place the bowl over a saucepan half filled with boiling water. Continue beating until the mixture starts to thicken. Remove from the heat. Dissolve the gelatine in 2 tablespoons of hot water. Allow it to cool before adding to the milk. Sweeten to taste and add the vanilla essence. Pour into a freezing tray and freeze until it sets around the edges. Remove from the freezer (or freezing compartment) and beat in a chilled bowl, until smooth. Pour the ice cream back into the freezing tray and return to the freezer. Leave it to set.

Variations

Omit the vanilla essence and add instead:

Coffee and nut: 2 tablespoons instant coffee and 25 g (1 oz) crushed roasted almonds.

Fruit: 450 g (1 lb) sieved fruit (strawberries, apricots, etc.).

Carob: 2 tablespoons carob powder heated with a pinch of cinnamon in 2 tablespoons water. Cool before adding to the mixture.

Parsley water ice

2 tablespoons finely chopped parsley	1 tablespoon dry sherry
juice and grated rind of 1 lemon	250 ml (½ pint) water
1 egg white	liquid artificial sweetener to taste

Heat the lemon juice and rind with the water until boiling. Stir in the parsley and simmer for a few minutes. Remove from the heat and leave to cool. Stir in the sherry and add the sweetener. Pour the mixture into a freezing tray and place in the freezer or freezing compartment of the fridge. Whisk the egg white until stiff and beat it into the ice when the crystals start to form. Return to the freezer and leave to harden.

Variations

Omit parsley, lemon juice and sherry and add instead:

Grapefruit and mint: juice of 1 grapefruit and 2 tablespoons chopped mint.

Raspberry and rosewater: 450 g (1 lb) puréed raspberries mixed with 3 tablespoons rosewater.

Mango and yoghourt ice cream

1 large tin, 822 g (1 lb 13 oz) mango pulp	1 large carton, 454 g (16 fl oz) yoghourt

Mix the mango pulp with the yoghourt in a chilled bowl. Pour it into a freezing tray and place in the freezer or freezing compartment of the fridge. Remove from the freezer and beat at regular intervals to ensure that it sets to a smooth texture.

Variations

Omit the mango pulp and add instead:

Lemon: the juice and rind of 2 lemons.

Carob: 2 tablespoons carob powder heated in the juice of 1 orange and cooled.

Redcurrant: 450 g (1 lb) puréed redcurrants, cooked with 2 tablespoons honey, a pinch of sweet cicely and a little water, and cooled.

Index

Book Tokens

**Give them
the pleasure of choosing**

Book Tokens can be bought
and exchanged at most
bookshops in Great Britain
and Ireland.